Oct. 28/05

Dear Mom

Hope you have lots of the
enjoying reading about the
old times in Saanich & that
you're feeling better really soon.

Love,
Glenda & Arthur
XO

Saanich

Centennial

1906-2006

100 years - 100 stories

Library and Archives Canada Cataloguing in Publication

Saanich centennial, 1906-2006 : 100 years, 100 stories.

Edited by Valerie Green and Geoffrey Castle.

ISBN 0-9694072-2-X

1. Saanich (B.C.)--Biography. 2. Saanich (B.C.)--History.
I. Green, Valerie, 1940- II. Castle, Geoffrey, 1930- III. Saanich (B.C.)

FC3845.S22S24 2005   971.1'28   C2005-906124-3

Printed in Canada by
First Choice Books
#2 – 460 Tennyson Place
Victoria, British Columbia V8Z 6S8
www.firstchoicebooks.ca

The Saanich Centennial Book Committee would like to dedicate this book to the youth of Saanich – many of whom will participate in the stewardship of the future of the Municipality.

Front cover:
(top row) Vantreight Family Portrait *(Saanich Archives)*; Girls racing on McMorrans Beach, 1912 *(Saanich Archives)*; W.D. Michell's potato crop *(Saanich Archives)*; Norm Baker *(Courtesy Nancy Baker)*; Reeve Quick outside the old Royal Oak Inn *(Saanich Archives)*
(2nd row) W.W. Gibson's plane *(Saanich Archives)*; Mr McMorran blasting stumps on Broadmead Farm *(Saanich Archives)*; Nellie Furtado *(Courtesy Island Publishers Newsgroup)*; Broadmead Farm *(Saanich Archives)*; Bill Turner *(Courtesy The Land Conservancy of BC)*
(3rd row) Nellie McClung *(Saanich Archives)*; Mr Borden Senior in a car with a feed salesman *(Saanich Archives)*; Silken Laumann *(Courtesy S. Laumann)*; Dr Plaskett with the completed telescope *(Saanich Archives)*
(bottom row) Giff Calvert *(Courtesy Lissa Calvert)*; Katherine, Isobel and Ruth Goward *(Saanich Archives)*; Ken Middleton *(Saanich Archives)*; Roy Vickers *(Courtesy Times Colonist)*

Back Cover:
(top right) First Saanich Municipal building, Glanford Avenue (demolished)
(top left) 1911 Saanich Municipal Hall, 4512 West Saanich Road
(main photo) Saanich Municipal Hall, 770 Vernon Avenue, 1965 to present

Table of Contents

FOREWORD v

INTRODUCTION vii

Foreword

Saanich was incorporated on March 1st, 1906. The first meetings took place in a small house on Glanford Avenue that was rented for five dollars per month and there were actually more Council members than municipal staff. The police force consisted of one constable who patrolled 70 square miles on horseback. Fire protection depended on volunteers and the neighbouring Victoria department.

Saanich has grown from these modest beginnings with a population of less than 5,000 to over 110,000 citizens today. Residents now enjoy a full range of municipal services that make the community a desirable place to live, work and play.

Many of our community's structures are recognized and protected for their heritage value, including our present Municipal Hall, so that they are preserved as part of Saanich's future. This book focuses on significant Saanich citizens – one hundred lives representing one hundred years – and these stories describe their contributions to our community and preserve the legacy they leave.

I am also pleased to note that our Saanich Police and Fire Departments are represented within as well as those worthy citizens who have been awarded the Freedom of Saanich.

Rotary International is our partner in this endeavour and we thank the three Rotary Clubs in Saanich for their work with this book and their work in our community.

I commend this special centennial book to you on behalf of Saanich Councils, past and present, as we recommit one of the oldest municipalities in British Columbia to our motto: POPULO SERVIENDO – SERVING THE PEOPLE.

Mayor Frank Leonard

Introduction

Early in 2004, a committee was formed to discuss ideas for ways to celebrate Saanich's Centennial. Mayor Frank Leonard suggested that it might be a good idea to write a book of one hundred biographies of people both past and present closely identified with the development and enhancement of the municipality.

It was decided to loosely group the biographies into ten-year periods beginning with 1906, the year that Saanich was formed. The committee then had to determine which must be included. Not every reader will concur with the committee's choices, which, with one exception, excluded Saanich employees. Another criterion was the subjects should be long-time residents of Saanich.

Selections became a challenge but much of the biographical material was researched in the Saanich Archives. Others, placed mainly in the more recent decades, were written using information obtained elsewhere.

From among some 12,000 images, the Saanich Archives could provide only half the required photographs. More were located and obtained from other archival institutions, private individuals and from the press.

The book went to the printers in September, 2005 and the information and the interviews were placed in the Saanich Archives, where they are available to researchers during the hours of 9:00 a.m. to 12:30 p.m., Monday through Friday.

Saanich Centennial Book Committee:

> Paul McKivett, Chairman
> Bill Bryant, Co-Chair and Saanich Rotary Representative
> Geoffrey Castle, Archivist and Editor
> Valerie Green, Author and Editor
> Caroline Duncan, Archives Research Assistant and Photographic Coordinator
> Lindsey Norris, University of Victoria Creative Writing Student (Biographer)
> Michelle Simms, University of Victoria Creative Writing Student (Biographer)
> Tracy Ryan, Publicist
> Isobel Hoffmann, Secretary

While the information in this book is believed to be accurate, we realize that it is not always possible to authenticate some information obtained from interviews and other sources. Therefore, in striving to keep the record correct, we welcome comments from readers.

Freemen of Saanich

Throughout history, municipalities, towns and cities have honoured their distinguished citizens by bestowing upon them the title of "Freeman" to recognize accomplishments, contributions and outstanding service to the community. Much like being given a key to the city, being named a Freeman is the highest honour a municipality can grant, and must be passed by a unanimous vote of members of the municipal council. Originally, the title came with considerable power, as Freemen had tax, trading and voting privileges. They were therefore powerful in local government. Today, Freemen are listed at the top of the voters list, and are permitted to vote and run for mayor regardless of where they reside. Since incorporation, Saanich has honoured eight residents and two groups with Freeman status.

General G.R. Pearkes
July 12, 1968

Major General George Randolph Pearkes is fitting as the first Freeman named in Saanich. As a war hero, politician and Lieutenant Governor

Lt. Gov. George and Mrs Pearkes receiving the Freedom of Saanich, 1968 (Saanich Archives 1981-21-9)

of B.C., he served his community and country throughout his lifetime. George Pearkes came to Canada from England in 1888, where the 18-year-old first homesteaded in the Rocky Mountain area before moving north to the Yukon with the Royal Northwest Mounted Police. In March of 1915, he joined the Canadian Mounted Rifles, and would then make the army his life until the conclusion of WWII. While serving in France, he advanced up to Lt. Colonel, and later commanded the 116th Battalion. He was wounded in action five times, and was awarded the D.S.O. , the Military Cross and the Victoria Cross for his bravery.

After settling in Saanich, George turned his ambitions to the political arena, and served as Minister of National Defense in the Diefenbaker administration, and later represented the Nanaimo and Esquimalt/Saanich ridings in the House of Commons. As much as he was known for his staunch conservative politics, George was also known for his involvement in community projects, such as the G.R. Pearkes Centre for Children. He was sworn in as Lieutenant Governor of B.C. for two terms, from 1960 until his retirement in 1967, when he returned to Saanich to live with his wife, Constance Blytha at their house on Tattersall Drive until his death in 1984 at age 96.

Constance Blytha Pearkes
July 12, 1968

Blytha Pearkes was named a Freeman of Saanich on July 12, 1968, the same day as her famous husband. Born in Cochrane, Alberta, in

1902, her family moved west to Vancouver in 1906, then to Sidney two years later. While her husband served as Lieutenant Governor, Mrs. Pearkes was known for her charm and hospitality as Chatelaine of Government House, where she entertained Royalty, foreign Ambassadors, and thousands of the general public. During her years in the public eye, she was named the Knights of Columbus Victoria Citizen of the Year in 1967 for her devotion to the community. Mrs. Pearkes served as Honourary President of numerous voluntary health organizations and service groups, and was a Life Member of the Women's Auxiliary of the Anglican Church of Canada.

Freeman Ford King (Skipper)
January 12, 1973

"Skipper" King (Courtesy Times Colonist)

Long before newspapers reported the dangers of global warming, Freeman "Skipper" King

was educating both children and adults about the importance of preserving the environment. For decades Skipper inspired a responsibility to the environment in the legions of visitors to Goldstream Park who attended his nature programs. Born in Sussex, England, Skipper came to Canada as a seaman when he was 18. Throughout his long career, he was responsible for the creation of many parks, including the John Dean Park in North and Central Saanich, McDonald Park in North Saanich and Eves Park near Duncan. More important than his work in the field, however, was Skipper's ability to inspire others. Environmentalist Briony Penn credits much of her love of nature to her sessions spent in the park with him.

To honour Skipper, and create opportunities for young people to continue and initiate projects in line with his devotion to nature conservation, the Freeman F. King Scholarship fund was established. The Scholarship, awarded each year to a fourth-year Biology student at the University of Victoria, is a way for Skipper's devotion to the environment to continue.

Leslie Henry Passmore
January 31, 1975

As a former Reeve and Councillor who served for more than three decades, Leslie H. Passmore was influential in creating many of the policies and structures that exist in Saanich today. He was instrumental in bringing affordable housing and sewage systems to the community, and in the abolishment of the ward system, which he believed was parochial because farmers were paying taxes for services they would never use, but the urban citizens wanted. Though frequently controversial and outspoken, Les always said he had opponents, not enemies. Former Mayor Ed Lum described him as a kind and dedicated man, and a champion of the underdog.

In 1977, he was chairman of the Royal Oak Cemetery Board, sat on the Advisory Planning Commission and was on the Board of Variance. He served his last term as Councillor in 1974 at age 76. His retirement was marked by Leslie Passmore Day, with a community picnic held at Beaver Lake Park.

Les Passmore (Saanich Archives 1981-4-18)

Dr. Hugh L. Keenleyside
March 17, 1985

Throughout his years of service to Canada, Dr. Hugh L. Keenleyside earned a reputation for his concern for the betterment of the human race, and his commitment to humanitarian issues. Born in Toronto in 1898, Hugh moved to Vancouver with his family where he spent his youth. After returning from the First World War he was one of the first graduates at the University of British Columbia, which he followed with an M.A. and Doctorate from Clark University. He began his

career teaching history at many universities in the United States and at U.B.C.. Following his academic career, Hugh worked for the Federal Civil Service as third secretary in the Department of External Affairs. He opened Canada's first diplomatic mission in Japan in 1929, which was the first extension of Canada's foreign relations outside of the United States. He led a Canadian delegation to the United Nations where he was administrator of technical assistance for developing nations. In later years, as a Canadian and United Nations diplomat, Hugh would help foster Canada's diplomatic reputation and strongly campaigned for nuclear disarmament.

Among the many accolades Hugh received throughout his life, he was named not only a Freeman of Saanich, but of Vancouver as well. He won the Pearson Peace Medal in 1982 and was the first recipient of the Vanier Medal from the Institute of Public Administration in 1962. He was made a Companion of the Order of Canada in 1969. When Hugh was made a Freeman of Saanich in 1985 he had lived in the municipality with his wife Katherine for 25 years. Here, he served as first president of the Horticulture Centre of the Pacific and first chairman of the Saanich committee on bravery awards, and surprised friends by winning a local baking contest with a home-made mince pie. W.A.C Bennet described Hugh as "One of the brightest minds in Canada… a man whose record reads like the record of a dozen men."

Bruce Hutchison
May 27, 1990

Bruce Hutchison had the longest journalism career in Canadian history, which began on April 12, 1918, when the 16-year-old presented himself at the office of the Victoria Times Daily, where he would soon earn $12 per week as a sports writer. As the years passed, Bruce's interests broadened; he gained a reputation as one of the most perceptive political commentators in Canadian journalism, making him both admired and despised by countless politicians across the country. Bruce's opinions were widely cited, sometimes on the floor of the House of Commons. In 1952, members of the B.C. Legislature were so outraged by one of his opinions in the Victoria Times that they came within a few votes of summoning his publisher before the bar of the House to apologize. Hutchison responded by reprinting the offending editorial on the front page, just in case anyone missed it the first time, and in a follow-up piece he congratulated the legislators on having so narrowly avoided making themselves look "ridiculous". (The offending editorial was one of a series that won its author the National Newspaper Award for 1952.)

Bruce Hutchison receiving the Freedom of Saanich, 1990
(Saanich Archives 1990-28-18)

Bruce's writing was not limited to Canadian politics. He wrote some of Canada's enduring classics, including *The Unknown Country*, winner of the Governor General's Award for non-fiction in 1942; *The Incredible Canadian*, a biography of Mackenzie King, which won the same award a decade later; *The Far Side of the Street*, his autobiography, and *The Fraser*, described as one of the most readable journeys into early B.C. History.

Kenneth William Middleton
June 14, 1992

Ken Middleton, "Mr Saanich"
(Saanich Archives 1992-25-43)

Ken Middleton began his career with Saanich in 1947, when Saanich was primarily a rural municipality. As a Junior Clerk in the Tax Department, he quickly rose to become Senior Clerk and later Chief Cashier and Collector of Taxes. When he retired in 1992, Ken had served the community for 45 years, setting a record for the longest serving staff member in Saanich history. Known as "Mr. Saanich," Ken was always willing to give a hand, and was always dedicated to his community. Listing the numerous committees and organizations Ken was involved with, it becomes clear that Saanich was not just an employer and home to Ken. He made Saanich a part of his life, and a better place in which to live.

Outside his duties in the Clerks office, Ken was a member of the Saanich Special Events Committee for almost 30 years, and a member of the Municipal Hall Safety Committee. He served on the executive of the Vancouver Island Chapter of the Municipal Officers' Association, and the Municipal Officers' Association of British Columbia. He spent over 25 years with the Civil Defense Program and acted as coordinator of the Emergency Feeding Program. When a call for the Emergency Feeding Vehicle came, Ken and his family would be there no matter what time of day or night, always with a smile and encouraging word for those working in the emergency situation. Ken and his wife Ev were avid square dancers, serving on the executive of their club, The Country Cousins, and as editors of the Cross Trail News, the official publication for square dancing on Vancouver Island. Ken died after suffering a heart attack at the Municipal Hall in November, 2003.

In 1994, two groups were given the Freeman status. Not an honour given lightly, bestowing Freeman status on the 11 (Victoria) Service Battalion and 11 (Victoria) Medical Company granted the groups the right to bear arms and privilege of marching through the streets of Saanich in full dress with bayonets fixed.

11 (Victoria) Service Battalion
April 9, 1994

The 11 (Victoria) Service Battalion was formed in 1970 and is descended from 155 Company Royal Canadian Army Service Corps. The role of the Service Battalion is to supply an administrative headquarters, transportation, maintenance, food service and military policing for Victoria. Mayor Coell said during the presentation council meeting that the 11-Service Battalion performs in the best traditions of the service. "A volunteer in the service of our country is twice the citizen…To be a volunteer in the service of one's country is an honourable profession." The soldiers who form the Battalion come from all walks of life on Vancouver Island, and became part of the Saanich municipality in 1991 when the Armoury was moved from Bay street to the former Gray Bottling and Beverage Depot. While carrying out operations the 11-Service Battalion provides combat service to support a brigade, and many personnel from the unit have served

in the former Yugoslavia, Cyprus and the Middle East. By recognizing the Battalion, Saanich demonstrated the esteem with which its members are held.

11 (Victoria) Medical Company
September 24, 1994

The 11 (Victoria) Medical Company lives up to the former Medical Corps motto: "Faithful in Adversity". The unit is the successor to the 13th Field Ambulance of World War I and II, and is one of 14 Primary Reserve medical units across Canada. The unit participates in provincial and national exercises and competitions, and has won the Provincial Military First Aid Shield, and both the Ryerson and Shillington Trophies which are awarded to the two top units in the national Militia Medical competitions. The mission of the Company is to train part-time soldiers to provide emergency medical care in an Army environment, "a role in many instances no less dangerous than those of the combat arms," said Mayor Coell at the presentation council meeting. Many soldiers serving in the Medical Company wear medals for their involvement as peacekeepers, and the title of Freeman recognizes the civilian volunteers for their service to our country.

Hugh Austin Curtis
March 23, 2002

Born and raised on southern Vancouver Island, Hugh Austin Curtis was named a Freeman of Saanich on September 24, 1994, for his long career in public service and dedication to his community and province. Hugh graduated from Victoria High School, and immediately embarked on his career as a radio announcer. He worked for C-FAX until 1961, but even early on, it was clear that Hugh had an interest in public service. In his teens, he produced *Spotlight on Youth*, a teenage radio talent series, and helped organize Sunday evening theatre rallies for Red Cross Blood Donations. At C-FAX, Hugh worked in all areas of broadcasting, from on-air announcing to sales, promotion and management. For his talents and work ethic, Hugh was awarded the John G. Gillin Jr. Memorial award for public service radio series.

Hugh's father Austin Curtis had served in local government for 25 years, so few were

Mayor Hugh Curtis (Saanich Archives 1981-21-6)

surprised when he was elected to Council in 1961 for two terms, then elected Reeve in 1964 for three consecutive terms. While serving in 1968, the term Reeve was changed to Mayor, making Hugh Saanich's first Mayor. During his years of service, Hugh was also first Chair of the Capital Regional District, President of the Union of B.C. Municipalities, Vice President for B.C. of the Canadian Federation of Mayors and Chairman of the Municipal Finance Authority.

A major change during Hugh's years as Mayor was the creation of the Urban Containment Boundary, which helped preserve rural areas in Saanich. He also instituted the Sewer Enterprise program, allowing the installation of major sanitary sewer systems. He was instrumental in the acquisition of land, and was committed to the expansion of parks, open space and recreation facilities.

Hugh was elected to the British Columbia legislature in 1972, and in his seven years in Provincial politics he would work for Municipal Affairs and Housing, Government Services, and the Treasury Board. During his service as a Cabinet Minister he was responsible for B.C. Transit, B.C. Assessment Authority, Provincial Cabinet Commission, Islands Trust, B.C. Lottery Corporation, Sport B.C., and B.C. Provincial Museum, among others. Outside his political service, Hugh dedicated his time and energy to the Variety Club of B.C., the David Foster Foundation and served as Honourary Director of the B.C. Liberties Association.

11 (Victoria) Medical Company receiving the Freedom of Saanich (Saanich Archives 1995-6-19)

11 (Victoria) Medical Company (Saanich Archives 1995-6-23)

Serving the Community since 1906
SAANICH POLICE DEPARTMENT

Hugh Little on a Police horse, 1914
(Saanich Archives 1981-7-39a)

Over the past century, the Saanich Police Department has experienced much growth and development. After the municipality's incorporation in 1906, the department began with a single Officer, Constable Russell, who operated from home and patrolled the municipality on horseback. At the time, Saanich was organized into six wards initially which were predominantly agricultural and rural, except Ward Seven (added later) which was populated by Victorians who crossed into Saanich to escape the higher taxes in the city.

When E.F. Dawson became Chief Constable in 1911, new municipal offices were built at 4515 West Saanich Road, and by this time the department had grown to five Officers as well as Special Constables, who served when required. In 1915, the Specials were replaced with two full-time Constables. That year, Hugh Little was appointed Chief and the first official police uniform was adopted. The sight of the Saanich Constables, riding horseback in their high-necked khaki tunics, riding breeches, leather leggings and hat prompted the Victoria Police to nickname them "the Saanich Cowboys". The nickname wouldn't stick though; later that year, Saanich purchased a new Ford Passenger, the department's first police car, and in 1918 the horses were replaced by bicycles after a study revealed that the cost of oats for the horses ($22.50 per annum) was much higher than the $5 maintenance fee for the police bicycles. During these years, Chief Little was succeeded by Chief Constable James Dryden whose replacement, Robert Stevenson Brown, is remembered as one of the last Officers to patrol on horseback.

Constable Ken Cummings on a new motorcycle in 1936
(Saanich Archives 1981-7-20)

The first Police Ball was held in 1921, with all profits directed to several worthy charitable organizations. As the effects of the Great Depression took their toll, Saanich found it difficult to maintain public services. While some municipalities contracted with the B.C. Provincial Police, (now the RCMP), Chief Peter Brogan and the Police Commission decided that the best interests of Saanich residents would be served by asserting the independence of the department. A new uniform was adopted that year, the blue dress recognizable today. Brogan was followed by Thomas Hastings in 1926, then Alan Rankin who had joined the force in 1917 as a Special Constable.

Community services have always been of great importance, and in 1928 the department initiated the first school safety program. By this time, the department consisted of a Chief Constable, a Sergeant and three Constables. All Officers resided in the area they policed and were on duty 24 hours each day—true community policing ! By 1938, when Josiah Bull Jr. became Chief, the department had grown to 20 Constables and now included two cars equipped with radios. Following World War Two, servicemen who had trained in Victoria returned to the area to settle with grants secured under the Veterans Land Act. The influx of new residents began to shift Saanich's rural landscape into a more urban one, placing a stain on police services. The population continued to grow throughout the 1950s. In 1957, Chief Bull retired and was replaced by W.A. Pearson. During Pearson's years as Chief, the department grew to 70 Constables and moved into larger but temporary facilities on Viewmont Avenue before moving to the present location at Swan Lake. In 1960 the department and community mourned the death of Constable Robert Kirby, who was killed in the line of duty.

The Police Department saw many staff changes throughout the 1960s and 1970s. Chief Pearson was replaced by Bob Peterson, who was followed by John Post, then William Nixon. By the time James Arnold became Chief in 1996, the department employed over 200 staff, serving the largest community on Vancouver Island. Today, Chief Derek Egan oversees a department that still abides by its mission statement: "to provide the highest calibre of Police services in order to improve the quality of life in the Municipality of Saanich."

Police car fleet outside the Municipal Hall, 1947 (Saanich Archives 1983-3-49)

Leaders in Public Safety
SAANICH FIRE DEPARTMENT

At the time of Saanich's incorporation in 1906, the city of Victoria provided fire protection for the entire region.

In 1917, after 11 years of depending on Victoria, council responded to pressure from citizens, and rented a building on Douglas Street near Carey Road that would serve as a fire hall, equipped with 1,000 feet of fire hose and a single motor truck. The building rented for $7.50 per month, and was only wired for electricity in 1919. John G. Little was appointed "Fireman in Charge" at the department's inauguration in March of that year. Within the first year, John and his crew responded to 25 calls. By 1929, the municipality had replaced the old truck, and H.T. Lock was appointed Saanich's first official

Fire Chief.

Though Saanich now had its own department, fire protection was nowhere near the level required by the community. At the time, Saanich had only 170 fire hydrants, and still just the single truck. Fortunately, the department was about to rapidly expand. In 1938, a second truck was purchased and two years later, another truck and vehicle were obtained. Chief Joseph Law led seven employed firefighters, and at larger fires, the public works staff could be called on to assist. As Saanich continued to develop, more fire stations were needed to

protect the growing community. The second fire hall was built at Elk Lake in 1947, but was relocated to Royal Oak in 1978. The third fire hall was constructed on Shelbourne Street in 1950, to accommodate the developing Gordon Head and Cadboro Bay districts.

Along with more buildings to protect came a much larger population base. The fire department responded by introducing new services. The ambulance service began in the 1960s, and in 1961, the fire and police departments moved into new quarters at 760 Vernon Avenue, where they remain to this day. Chief Law retired in 1964 and was replaced by Joe Sutherland, who was succeeded by Glen Robbins in 1971. Glen, who had been Deputy Chief for 22 years retired after 11 months and was followed by Harold Gaines and then R.A. Fryer.

This was the beginning of a new era in the Saanich Fire Department. During the 1970s, Saanich was recognized as a leading fire department in the ambulance and rescue field. It was the first in Canada to administer drugs and incorporate special life support equipment to aid heart attack victims. The Life Pak installed in the ambulance could monitor the patient's heart beat and transmit the EKG directly to the Royal Jubilee Hospital. To ensure all officers were well-trained and kept up to date on the new services and equipment in use, the department introduced a new position: a full-time training officer, which

was relatively unheard of at the time. Anyone wishing to pursue Officer ranks was required to write promotional exams as the department remained dedicated to providing the highest possible levels of service. During this decade, the No. 3 fire station opened at the University of Victoria on McKenzie Avenue, Saanich introduced a Prevention and Inspection division, and the Water Rescue and Safety program was established.

As Saanich continued to grow through the 1980s and 1990s, Prevention and Inspection programs expanded to include a school fire safety program. Chief Fryer retired in 1984, and was replaced by Orville McGregor and then Dave Hill, who had started with the department as an alarm room operator in 1965. Dave was committed to fire prevention, and helped bring in the smoke alarm bylaw. Murray Bryden took over as Chief in 1997. Saanich purchased Sierra Fox, a 22-foot rigid-hull Zodiac, equipped with a GPS unit and a small hose and pumper. Sierra Fox allows the department to assist with sea rescues. A self-propelled trailer was built for the zodiac by members of the department, to make it capable of climbing over logs. This innovative piece of equipment has drawn interest from around the world. Ron Cullis took over as Chief in 2002 and was followed by Dave Ward, Saanich's current Fire Chief, in 2004. Today, the department has 103 career firefighters and five support personnel.

photos on previous page:

top: Saanich's first fire truck (Saanich Archives 1980-4-1)
middle: No. 1 Fire Hall, Douglas Street (Saanich Archives 1978-1-18)
bottom: No. 2 Fire Hall, Hamsterly Road (Saanich Archives 1985-3-1)

Making hay, c1915 (Saanich Archives
1981-12-10)

Gorge Regatta, early 1900s
(Saanich Archives 1981-13-4)

1906 - 1915

On March 1, 1906, Saanich was incorporated as a municipality with 18,200 hectares of land. Pioneers who had developed agriculture on the peninsula had begun a tradition of balancing urban and rural life by selling their produce within the city of Victoria while maintaining independence from merchant domination, a spirit that has influenced the lives of Saanich residents to this day. Within two days of incorporation, six councilors led by reeve Thomas Brydon began to hold council meetings in the Hilliger house.

Soon, the first of the Saanich land booms was underway with nurseries, dairies and farms covering much of the peninsula. Blenkinsop Road was built in 1906, and two years later Saanich was divided into six, and later seven, wards. To accommodate the population increase, building development was constant in Saanich's early years, including the first Gordon Head subdivision, the Appleton Property. In its first municipal decade, Saanich saw the early flight of William Wallace Gibson's twin plane in 1910, and the establishment of a rural mail route. Water towers were erected to service farms until the Saanich Waterworks reached rural areas, and schools were built. Craigflower School, the oldest surviving school building in Western Canada, completed in 1855, was used until 1911 when a new two-room structure was built across the street. That same year, council meetings were moved to the new municipal hall at Royal Oak. Wilkinson Road Jail, built in 1912, held prisoners of war and offenders against the Naval Discipline Act.

While transportation in the region had been improved by the completion of the Victoria and Sidney Railway in 1894, competition arrived on June 13, 1913 when the B.C. Electric Railway began operation. During the 1914-1918 War, Canadian Northern Pacific Railway (later CN) constructed a line from Victoria to Patricia Bay. The three lines served a Saanich population of less than 10,000. The Normal School opened on January 14, 1915. It is now a part of the Lansdowne campus of Camosun College.

Rosebank Farm, 1892 (Saanich Archives 1980-17-1)

Long Gun Jack

JACK IRVINE

Jack "Long Gun"Irvine: 1861 - 1948
Alice Whittaker: 1863-1939

In 1873, 12-year-old Jack Irvine and an old HBC flintlock rifle were competing against men with modern guns for a Christmas turkey. Turkey shoots were regular occurrences in Esquimalt around Christmas, and for 50-cents, anyone could try to nab a turkey or a goose. While Jack had shot rabbits, bears and other game with the old gun, experienced men with modern guns were another matter.

But Jack won five out of five turkeys, and

was eventually barred from competing, since the officers claimed his long gun gave him an advantage. From then on, he was known as "Long Gun Jack."

Jack's parents, John and Jessie Irvine, came from the Orkneys in 1851 to work for the Hudson's Bay Company. When they fulfilled their contract, they bought land in Portage Inlet, where Jack was born in 1861. Later, the Irvines settled in the Cedar Hill district on Rose Bank farm. The original property was 100 acres, but would eventually grow to be over 300.

In 1942, Jack completed his memoir: *Early Victoria: Reminiscences of Jack "Long Gun"*

Irvine. Though he admitted that he occasionally got dates wrong and had a reputation as a "story teller," his 200-page memoir has become a valuable reference for historians.

Jack wrote that by the time he was nine, he "had to be a man and do quite a few jobs on the farm such as milking cows, feeding sheep, cleaning up cow sheds, etc. Anyhow, it helped to quiet me down quite a bit, and there wasn't so much skylarking at school, of course there was usually the carpet tack on the teacher's chair or some such innocent little thing as you might expect from such nice kids."

Jack and mischief weren't an infrequent combination; when he was nine, he caught his hand in a chaff cutter, and turned two of his fingers into "sausage meat." When he was finally taken to the doctor, he and his wife were having breakfast; so the wife gave Jack toast and eggs to eat while Dr. Trimble mended his hand. Though Jack lost the joints, his fingers were saved, and he wrote that it was "the first time in Victoria that boiled eggs were used as an anaesthetic."

Jack was 16 when he became a clerk at a grocery store/saloon. After he made enough money, he married Alice Whittaker in 1883 and they went on to have four children.

He learned the dairy farm trade from William Tolmie on Braefoot farm before starting his own farm at Rose Bank. He farmed for 20 years before becoming a road foreman for the Saanich Municipality, earning $3 a day, until a fall and the resulting back injury prevented him from returning to work.

The honest, humorous voice of his memoirs reveals the colourful characters in Victoria and Saanich, and goes beyond factual details to capture a three-dimensional period of time.

For example, when he discusses Lord John Russell, the man who introduced the handsome cab to Victoria, Jack writes, "I never knew why he was called Lord John Rus[s]ell for, but as long as I knew him that was what he was called. I think it was because he put on lots of airs."

Thanks to Long Gun Jack, Lord Russell's airs, the turkey shoots and egg anaesthetics are immortalized as part of Saanich's history.

The Colony Hangman

MATTHIAS ROWLAND

Joseph William Rowland (son of Matthias Rowland) and wife
Euphemia (Saanich Archives 1985-1-2)

Matthias Rowland: 1823 – 1903
Elizabeth Rowland

Before public executions were outlawed in 1870, they served as a form of macabre entertainment, and whole crowds of people would gather in Bastion Square to see the accused swing from the gallows. Matthew Begbie was known as the "hanging judge". However, there is no real evidence to support this misnomer.

Hangmen could earn as much as 10 pounds per execution, a figure more than half of what the average farm labourer could expect in a year. But it was a gruesome and unpopular occupation, and men always wore hoods to protect their anonymity. If written records hadn't revealed that Matthias Rowland was the official hangman, people may never have known that the hotel proprietor, farmer and, at one point, the highest tax payer in Saanich, was the colony's hangman.

In November 1852, Peter Brown was tending a flock of sheep belonging to the Hudson's Bay Company (HBC) when he was shot and killed. Two months later, James Douglas responded to tips that one of the men responsible for the murder was a Cowichan native and the other was the son of a Nanaimo chief. He gathered 130 sailors and marines and sailed to Cowichan.

The HBC ship Recovery was greeted by over 200 warriors who were reluctant to turn the suspect over, as it was customary to exchange goods as recompense. But Douglas wanted to bring the man to trial, and eventually the tribe gave him up. After a long pursuit through the woods of Nanaimo, the second man was caught and both were tried on the deck of the steamship Beaver by a hastily convened jury. Both were sentenced to death. A gallows was erected at, appropriately, Gallows Point, and the men were executed in front of their tribes and families.

The grisly affairs of the Lake Hill murder have been carefully recorded in history books, but few of them mention the hooded man who played the crucial role. Rowland was born in Dorsetshire, England. When he was 30 years old he sailed around Cape Horn on the Norman Morison on the same voyage as Dr. J.S. Helmcken.

He and his wife, Elizabeth, raised six daughters and a son who all attended Craigflower school.

From 1850 to 1854 Rowland served as a steward on the Beaver, and later as a land labourer. In 1865 his contract with the HBC was completed and he settled on the farm known as Strawberry Vale, later called the Burnside Farm. At one point, his farm was over 500 acres, situated where the Pacific Forestry Centre and Tillicum Mall are today. The farm included beef cattle, dairy products, fruit and vegetables.

In the late 1880's Rowland opened the Burnside Hotel, which, as the only local watering hole in the area and with the advantage of being just north of the Esquimalt naval base, was extremely successful. He operated the hotel until approximately 1884, and other members of his family ran it until after 1905. But like his life as hangman, the hotel is shrouded in mystery – its exact opening and closing dates are not well documented.

If Matthias Rowland is not remembered for his hooded activities, he is remembered by Rowland Avenue, which runs parallel to Carey Road, and by Rowland Heights subdivision.

The Rowland Family in front of the Burnside Hotel, c1898 (Saanich Archives 1985-1-1)

A Prejudiced Society

CHARLES ALEXANDER

Charles Alexander: 1824 – 1913
Nancy Alexander: d.1911

In 1850, California was ostensively a free state, except that no black man could testify against a white man, any escaped slaved found in the state was arrested, and, by 1858, San Francisco schools were segregated and black children expelled. When Assemblyman A.G. Stokes drafted a bill proposing to "prohibit the immigration of free negroes and other obnoxious persons into this state and to protect and regulate the conduct of such persons now within the state," California's black population had heard enough. At the invitation of Governor James Douglas, nearly 700 people left their homes and headed north to Victoria in 1858.

The mass migration was a result of the Fraser River gold rush. It depleted Victoria of labour, and the growing American population in the city made Douglas fear for the continued existence of the British Colony. Aware of the discontent among the black community after slavery was upheld in 1857, Douglas counted on the Blacks to provide a counterbalance to the Americans.

Among the 700 people to immigrate was Saanich pioneer Charles Alexander. Charles was born in St. Louis, Missouri in 1824. In 1857, he and his wife Nancy traveled west to California in a covered wagon. On reaching California, Charles worked unsuccessfully in the gold mines. The family had arrived at the peak of anti-black feeling, so when they heard Douglas' invitation, they were one of the first families to make the voyage.

(Saanich Archives 1981-18-4)

When Charles arrived in BC, he went prospecting for gold on the Fraser River, with more success than he enjoyed in California. In 1861 he purchased a farm near Shady Creek. Charles was instrumental in the construction of the Shady Creek Methodist Church, and also became one of its first preachers. Standing more than six feet two inches tall and weighing more than 200 pounds, he offered his considerable carpentry skills to help build the first church and school in the district.

Charles also oversaw the construction of the Shady Creek United Church. There is a five-year gap in history that fails to explain why the Methodist congregation left the first church in 1890 and built a different church in 1895. One theory is that black families could be given land but it could never be properly registered, so the land could be taken over by white settlers – there may not be a record explaining the gap in the Church's history because no one wanted a record of it. As one minister said, kicking a congregation out of their church is "not exactly your most Christian thing to do." Supporting this theory is the fact that the Church was built on McMillian farm land, but there is no record of the McMillian farm, though they were another prominent family.

In his 33 years of living and farming in the Saanich area, Charles became a founding member of both the Temperance Society and the Saanich Agricultural Society. He and his wife had 12 children, and many descendants are still living in the Saanich area.

The historical gaps of the Shady Creek Churches reveal a greater flaw in the history of the municipality, of the province and of Canada. The black pioneers experienced the same hardships as white settlers, in addition to living in a society that was prejudiced, suspicious and occasionally outright hostile. And in the majority of cases, there are few records to remember either their successes or their sacrifices.

This biography has been sponsored by
The Saanich Sunrise Rotary Club
- meets for breakfast every Tuesday morning at 7:00 a.m.
at the de Dutch Pannekoek House at Quadra and McKenzie
Contact: Jan Brister at 381-2389

The First Settlers of Royal Oak

THE DURRANCE FAMILY

Mrs John Durrance, Senior
(Saanich Archives 1981-11-1)

John Durrance: 1828 - 1904
Jane Cheeseman Baily Durrance: d.1897

When the V&S northbound train was labouring under a particularly heavy load, it was so slow to climb the steep Royal Oak Hill that passengers would get off and walk to the lounge in the Royal Oak Inn. From there, they could sit in a comfortable chair and watch their train chug slowly up the hill.

The Royal Oak Inn was originally built to be the private residence of Richard and Jane Cheeseman, but fate would have other plans for the

dwelling. Richard came to Canada as a Hudson's Bay Company employee from Chatham, England. Two years later, he went back to England and married his childhood sweetheart, Jane Dyke.

The couple arrived back in Fort Victoria in January 1853. Richard exchanged his downtown property for 214 undeveloped acres five miles north of the fort, in the Royal Oak area. The Cheesmans began the process of clearing land for their house, which would become the Royal Oak Inn, where the present East and West Saanich Roads diverge.

Jane and Richard were the first settlers in the area, and Jane is usually credited with christening the place "Royal Oak," but there are several stories that explain how it got the name. In one tale, Jane was walking on the property on a hot day, and she stopped to rest in the shade of a large tree, and proclaimed it a royal oak. The other theory is that an old oak tree suddenly crashed to the ground while the hotel was under construction. This theory is the most popular, because the hotel burned to the ground in the 1890's, and some believe that the crashing tree was an ill omen.

Not long after the house was completed, Richard was killed when his horses bolted and threw him out of the wagon along the newly constructed Cheeseman Road. When Richard died, Jane was left with four children and 245 acres to look after. She continued to oversee the maintenance of the property for two years, before marrying James Bailey in 1864. During their marriage, they donated two acres for the old Royal Oak School. Bailey Road, which runs off West

Saanich Road, is named after James Bailey.

Jane's second husband died of heart trouble a few years after they married. A few months later, Jane married John Durrance, and she and her five children moved to "Spring Valley Farm" on the Saanich Peninsula.

John Durrance was born in 1828 in Leicestershire, England. He was 18 when he and his brother James left England. After landing in Canada they made a brief sojourn in California where James remained, but John came back to Vancouver Island.

In 1860, there were no roads to the north end of the Peninsula – the government wagon road ended at Elk Lake - so John first saw the land he wanted to purchase by canoe. He bought 385 acres in the present area of Durrance Road, next to the Rithet Farm; some of the land he purchased for only $1 an acre. He cleared as much as 50 acres by hand until he acquired a team of oxen, and lived in a tent until he could build a house. His first house was built near the corner of what are now Wallace Drive and Durrance Road.

In 1872, John and Jane Cheeseman Bailey Durrance had a son, also named John. In 1876 John purchased an additional 135 acres for $637. John Durrance Jr. married Nina (Daisy Webb) in 1903, and built a home west of his parents' farmhouse. They had four children, and John contin-

ued to run the Spring Valley Farm after his father died in 1904. The only things that remain of the farm now are the cherry trees planted by John Sr. on the corners of Wallace Drive and Durrance Road.

The inn, however, was not forgotten. In 1873, Louis Duval from Quebec bought the Royal Oak Hotel and a few years later he was living there with his wife Janie, who was Jane and Richard Cheesman's third daughter. When it burned down about 12 years later, Louis built a second hotel at the same sight. It opened for business in 1890.

The present Royal Oak Inn resort was built in 1960 by the four Isherwood brothers, and over the years has been expanded to its present form of 150 beds, complete with a pub, dining rooms, night club, lounge and golf course. The railway is gone as is the Inn, started more than a century ago by some of the first settlers of Royal Oak.

The Durrance Family (Saanich Archives 1981-11-4)

This biography has been sponsored by

Fernhill Financial

Aircraft built by W.W. Gibson, c1908 (Saanich Archives 1985-10-2)

Victoria's Birdman

WILLIAM WALLACE GIBSON

William Wallace Gibson: 1874 – 1965

On September 8, 1910, William Wallace Gibson flew the first all Canadian built aircraft at Saanich's Lansdowne field. The engine that he designed and built himself propelled his plane 20 feet above the ground and to a distance of 201 feet, over 70 feet longer than the 129 feet documented by the Wright Brothers in 1903.

Thirty-five-year-old Gibson accomplished this without any formal training or education in the field of aviation. In fact, almost everything about the operation was informal and unceremonious. The plane was built in Gibson's coach house at 146 Clarence Street in James Bay. The pilot's seat was a western stock saddle strapped to the plane's frame. The wings were 20-feet long and covered in blue silk; the undercarriage was four bicycle tires. The rudder was controlled

with a piece of rope. It was hauled to a grassy field on the Deans Farm near Mount Tolmie at 4 a.m., a time when no one was likely to see it.

When Gibson took his design to the Hutchinson brothers' Victoria Machinery Depot in Victoria and asked them to build the engine, they laughed at him and almost refused the job. At the time, anyone who wanted to fly was commonly regarded as crazy. Gibson was called the "Birdman," and often when he was walking down the street people would flap their arms at him and laugh. As a result of the public criticism, Gibson decided to make his first flight deep in the depths of Saanich – he didn't want to be ridiculed any more than he already had been for his "crazy" ideas.

Though Gibson had no formal aviation training, he had spent much of his youth flying kites and various contraptions – sometimes loaded

W.W. Gibson at his forge, c1905
(Saanich Archives 1985-10-3)

with hapless gophers – over the prairies. Born in Ayrshire, Scotland, he moved to Saskatchewan (then still a part of the Northwest Territories) when he was a child. One time he built a seven-foot kite, attached a basket to it and filled it with nine gophers. He flew the kite for over an hour, until it suddenly came crashing to the ground, killing all aboard. Some of his other designs were more successful; once he made a working model airplane using a window blind roller to propel it.

Gibson bought a gold mining claim on the Elk River on Vancouver Island for $500, which he later sold for $10,000 in 1907. This money financed his first airplane, the "Twinplane." After the Twinplane, he built the Multiplane, and moved to Delta, and later Calgary for its take-off friendly land.

Gibson crashed frequently, and often caused minor injuries to the pilot and major injuries to the plane. When his Multiplane was ready to be tested in 1911, his wife finally persuaded him to quit flying, and Gibson hired Alex Japp to pilot the plane. The "Multiplane" is now on display at the National Aeronautical Museum in Ottawa and a replica of the Twinplane is on display at the Saanich Air Museum. Gibson was also inducted into the B.C. Aviation Hall of Fame.

Despite Gibson's remarkable success and history-making achievement on the grassy meadow of the Dean farm, Victoria was curiously quiet about the occasion. Although he is now considered a pioneer of flight, Gibson received very little recognition during his lifetime. He eventually moved to the United States, and after a long career manufacturing mining machinery, died in California at age 91. Many years later, his son unveiled a plaque at Lansdowne Middle School in commemoration of his flight.

(Saanich Archives 1985-10-1)

Quick's Bottom

THE QUICK FAMILY

Reeve Quick at the old Royal Oak Inn, c1907 (Saanich Archives 1980-7-8)

Fredrick Quick: 1861 – 1927
William Quick: 1870 – 1952

Times have changed in Saanich. The population has increased exponentially, houses have overtaken the forests, and council meetings are no longer held in the homes of Saanich residents.

When Saanich was incorporated in 1906, council meetings were held in living rooms, initially in the Hilliger home or Pim farmhouse. But in 1911, thanks to the influence of William and Frederick Quick, a municipal hall was erected at 4512 West Saanich Road.

C.H. Merkly constructed and wired the building for a total cost of $4,652. This building served as the municipal hall until the current hall on Vernon Avenue, which cost approximately $800,000, was opened in 1965.

Fred and William were born in New Zealand, the two youngest sons of Christopher and Rebbeca Quick. Originally from Ireland, Christopher and Rebbeca moved to New Zealand shortly after they were married. They raised four children: Annie, Frank, Fred and William.

Annie was the first child to move to Vancouver Island with her husband. When her father's health began to fail, his doctor told him to move to a drier climate. Fred and William happened to be living in California at the time, so Christopher and Rebbeca took the doctor's advice, left New Zealand and joined their sons. Less than a year later, in 1889, the four of them moved to Vancouver Island.

Fred and William became involved in the dairy business and owned the first purebred herd of Jersey cows on Vancouver Island. They bought 150 acres off West Saanich and Wilkinson Roads and farmed for 35 years.

Frederick became very involved in public affairs. He was a councillor for Ward Four in 1907, Reeve of Saanich in 1908 and 1909, a councillor again in 1912 and re-elected as reeve in 1913. He married Agnes McGee-Murdock and had no children.

In 1909, William married Esther Carmichael. Esther was a founding member and one-time director of the Royal Oak Women's Institute. In 1913, they moved to 4512 Wilkinson Road where they raised three children.

Meanwhile, William and Esther were instrumental in convincing Saanich residents to build the Royal Oak Community Hall at 4516 West Saanich Road. John Durrance sold the land fairly cheaply, and twelve families contributed $100 dollars each. William then made up the difference. The hall was used for whist drives, basketball games and for various activities hosted by the Women's Institute. It was also used to hold Saanich council meetings before the new municipal hall was built.

People who don't remember the Quicks for their involvement with the municipal hall will probably recognize Quick's Pond or Quick's Bottom. Quick's Pond, at the corner of West Saanich and Wilkinson Roads, was named after William. Quick's Bottom was once part of the Quick farmland that is now a 33-acre wildlife sanctuary, an ideal spot for birdwatchers and one of the last remaining marshland areas in the Victoria area.

Quick's Bottom was purchased from the Quick family by the Saanich municipality in 1969, and in 1976 it was designated a wildlife sanctuary. Today, the area serves as important green space to citizens and a haven to rare and endangered species.

Follow the Cows to Saanich

THE PENDRAY FAMILY

Pendray's dairy herd, Saanich Road, 1967 (Saanich Archives 1978-1-51)

Follow the Birds To Victoria,
Follow the Cows to Saanich

William Joseph Pendray: d.1913
Amelia Carthew: d.1937, aged 87
John Carl Pendray: d.1961, aged 81

"If people are ever to become contented, happy and prosperous, they first must be made clean."

That was William Pendray's motto, and as the owner of the British America Soap Works in Victoria, he knew a great deal about both cleanliness and prosperity. The Pendray family was from Cornwall, England, and two distantly related branches settled in Victoria and Saanich in the early 20th century. One branch became involved in politics and business, the other into dairy farming.

After making a fortune panning for gold in the Cariboo, William Pendray went back to England to retire and promptly lost his fortune investing in South African gold mines. He returned to Vancouver Island, settling in Victoria in 1875. William noticed that thousands of dollars were being spent on imported soaps, while huge amounts of kitchen fat and tallow were thrown away on a daily basis. He decided to start a soap business in an abandoned building at the site that is presently the Empress Hotel. He manufactured every type of soap, from the harsh chemical soap used against lice, to perfumed toiletry soaps. After two years, he sent for his sweetheart in England, and in 1877 Amelia Carthew landed in Canada. They married that year.

In 1906, William bought a paint plant, BAPCO, and moved both businesses to Laurel Point. He was killed in an accident in his paint factory in 1913, and his son Carl decided to sell the soap business to the Lever Brothers, which has become one of the largest companies in North America.

Carl became the president of BAPCO, and married Florence Carter in 1903. Their main home was Loretto Hall (now Gatsbys) on Belleville

Street, but they also had a summer retreat at 5117 Cordova Bay Road, called "Rainbow Cottage," which is now a Saanich heritage house.

Carl was elected with an overwhelming majority as Mayor of Victoria in 1925, and served until 1928. He was also president of the Victoria Publicity Bureau, and was very involved in promoting Victoria as a tourist centre; in fact, he coined the well-known slogan, "Follow the Birds to Victoria." In 1958, he was awarded the Centennial Medal for outstanding service to the community.

At about the same time that Carl Pendray was turning the family paint business into a thriving success, Joseph and Charles Pendray were settling in the Swan Lake area of Saanich. Like William, the brothers were born in Cornwall. They moved to Victoria in the early 1900's and established dairy farms.

Joseph worked for the Municipality of Saanich in 1913. By 1917, he was operating a farm and renting grazing land on Christmas Hill and Greenridge. A year later, he bought land in Swan Lake, when only three or four houses existed in the area. By 1954, Joseph's son Thomas was running the 30-acre farm. The Swan Lake Dairy delivered whole raw milk directly to people's doors in quart bottles until 1978, long after most other dairies converted to the metric system and gave up the door-to-door delivery system.

In 1970, Saanich bought Thomas Pendray's farm for $112,375. Thomas continued to lease the land and run their family based home-delivery system for another eight years. The farm is now a part of the Swan Lake and Christmas Hill Nature Sanctuary. Charles Pendray, Joseph's brother, first purchased a small herd of cows and established a farm at Saanich and Falmouth Roads in 1912. Later, he moved to a larger farm on Blenkinsop Road and built up a dairy delivery route. He died in 1966 and his son John took over the farm.

John Pendray was born on the family dairy farm in Swan Lake in 1925. During the Second World War, farm help was extremely scarce and he had to decide whether he would quit school, or sell the delivery part of the business. He decided to do neither, and continued with his Grade 12 schooling while rising at 4 a.m. to get the deliveries done before he had to be at school. He continued this routine into his first two years at university, when he finally left school in favour of farming full-time.

In 1978, John realized the Blenkinsop Road farm was too small, so he purchased 185 acres on West Saanich Road. John Pendray was named Agriculturist of the Year in 1985 and was president of the Island Farms Dairies Cooperative Association for 29 years. His sons, David and Michael, are still operating the farm.

Together, the Pendray family had their hands in every major area of life: farming, politics, and business. Their homes have become heritage houses; their lands are parks and green spaces; their stories a part of community history. Whether through soap, paint, or milk, these pioneers improved the lives – and perhaps the smell – of people in Saanich and Victoria.

It Started With One Cow

ARTHUR LAMBRICK

Arthur, Clara and Elizabeth Lambrick
(Saanich Archives 1980-22-4)

Arthur Graham Lambrick: 1892 - 1967

Clara Eaton Sedgman: 1887- 1973

Arthur Lambrick didn't plan on being a dairy-man. When he bought a cow in 1913, he only wanted enough milk for his family, because he hated pasteurized milk. In fact, he called it "par-alyzed" milk, and believed that it was a health hazard.

He also did not originally plan to move to Saanich. He moved to Illinois from his birthplace in Cornwall, England, as a teenager, and on the ship back to England he met a boy who was returning from Victoria. That boy must have inspired him, because Lambrick left England and came to Victoria in 1911 when he was 19. He first worked in Fountain Shipyards, and later drove a truck for the Saanich municipality.

In 1914, Arthur married Clara Sedgeman and they had five chil-dren. When his first child was born he decided he didn't want his chil-dren raised on pasteurized milk, and bought that first cow. He also campaigned vigorously against the legislation that threatened to make pasteurization mandatory.

Though Arthur had no inten-tion of commercially supplying milk, his neighbours were contin-ually asking for it, so three years later Arthur bought a bigger piece of land at Shelbourne Street and Kings Road.

The family lived on Kings Road for a few years, until the first cow had multiplied into twenty. In 1924 Lambrick bought ten acres and a cottage from Luke Pither in Gordon Head, and drove his twenty cows down Shelbourne street to their new home. Over the years, Lambrick slowly acquired more of Pither's property and, in 1944, the Pither home.

Arthur Lambrick loved his cows and gave them all names. His herd continued to grow to 75, until at one point his farm was producing 160 gallons of milk a day. His employees reportedly liked him and he was a good employer, although unstinting in his demands for cleanliness.

Lambrick served as a councillor from 1935 to 1938 and reeve of Saanich from 1939 to 1940 and again in 1946. He was also chairman of the Vancouver Island Milk Producers' Association and a police commissioner.

In 1965 he sold 44.39 acres to Saanich for $263,000, which was far lower than market value. In 1969 10 acres was transferred to the School District and now houses Lambrick Park Secondary School. The park has become an indispensable addition to the community: its base-ball park has hosted the BC Summer Games, it has a skateboard park and it houses the Lambrick Community Centre.

Arthur may also have been right about raw milk. The pasteurization process, which heated the milk to 155 degrees Fahrenheit, made much of the crucial calcium insoluble. Some scientists have suggested pasteurized milk is more likely to carry diseases - including tuberculosis and listeriosis - than clean raw milk. His opposition to pasteurization and demands for cleanliness were controversial at that time.

Arthur Lambrick was not only a civil servant and a generous provider of recreational land. His raw-milk crusade provided citizens of Saanich with a choice regarding their health, an invaluable service for the community.

Bringing Music to the Backwoods

THE BUTLER FAMILY

Captain George Stephen Butler House, Keating Cross Road (Saanich Archives 1985-6-45)

Captain George Butler: 1834 – 1885
Fanny Catherine Brett: 1843 – 1920

Many Vancouver Island history books are dominated by men; men who cleared forests, established schools, became mayors and built railways. Often, the wives of these pioneers are barely discussed – but not in the Butler family. Fanny Butler, a wife, mother, schoolteacher and pianist, invested years of her life into tireless service for her family and the community, and was as essential as any other Saanich pioneer. As Danda Humphreys, local author and columnist, once wrote, "As far as the community was concerned, the Butlers were both welcome...but Fanny was nothing less than a godsend."

Captain George Butler and Fanny Brett were both born in Hampshire, England. George graduated from Oxford University, joined the army and served in the Crimean War. He was wounded and stationed in Quebec where he heard about the Cariboo Gold rush. He sold his commission and panned for gold in the Fraser River region for six years before settling in Victoria.

Butler mailed his marriage proposal to Fanny in England, and she must have accepted, because in 1868 she arrived in Victoria and they were married the next day.

Fanny was a governess and she became the first female schoolteacher in Saanich. She and George lived in the combination school and living quarters at Mount Newton Cross Road for several years, until a school was erected on the Turgoose property and they moved to West Saanich. The only time Fanny took time off from teaching was when she gave birth to one of her nine children.

In 1879 George acquired 160 acres in the centre of the Saanich Peninsula, on what is now Keating Cross Road. Fanny continued to teach while she raised the children and helped her husband farm. Also, Fanny's father had sent her a piano from England, and as the only piano in the district, the instrument was carted in a wagon all over the district – and with it, its pianist.

When George died in 1885 at age 51, Fanny had nine children to provide for: the oldest was sixteen and the youngest was two. She put her hard-travelled piano to work and gave lessons, turning her musical skills into a livelihood and passing on her love of music in the process.

It isn't only the Butler pioneers who are notable, either. Fanny and George's second-oldest son, Claude, started the Butler Brothers business in the 1940's. Claude and Pearl's eldest son saw the business into its expanded form of concrete and aggregate, and its incorporation in 1954.

Of Claude and Pearl's five children, four brothers continued running the business. It has survived the 30's depression, the 80's recession, and an exhausted gravel pit. It remains in operation today, and is considered one of the economic cornerstones of the Saanich community. It seems that Fanny Butler's investment has paid off. The Butler Brothers' business is still on the original homestead, and 50 acres are divided among various family members. The well-used piano was preserved and resides with the Saanich Pioneers Society. Many of Fanny's grandchildren also play the piano, which is probably the best possible memorial for the woman who brought music and education into the backwoods of Saanich.

Butler's Gravel Pit, Oldfield Road (Saanich Archives 1984-3-47)

This biography has been sponsored by
Berwick House – The Retirement Home that Set the Standard
4062 Shelbourne Street, Victoria, BC V8N 3E6   (250) 721-4062
www.berwickrc.com

The Pioneering Sluggetts

THE SLUGGETT FAMILY

John Sluggett at age 79 (Courtesy Larry Sluggett)

John Sluggett: 1829 - 1909
Fanny Down: 1835 – 1904

In 1867, much of Saanich was covered by thick forests of Cedar, Douglas Fir and Pine. Outside of Victoria, settlements were few, with only a handful of farms serving as outposts in the wilderness. One outpost belonged to the Sluggett family, whose presence marked the beginning of the community of Brentwood Bay. Not only did they own and farm two-thirds of the present area of Brentwood Bay, they also established a school, a church and the Sluggett Post Office. As it was an isolated patch of civilization on the Saa-

nich Peninsula, the BC Electric Railway called the area Sluggett Station.

Three weeks after John Sluggett married Fanny Down, they left their home in Devonshire, England, and immigrated to Canada. They farmed for over 20 years in Ontario. But John Sluggett wanted to get away from the long Ontario winters, so when he heard about the land opportunities and mild climate on Vancouver Island, he decided to make a visit. In 1876, a year after his first visit, he bought 704 acres for $7.50 an acre, and he and Fanny and their seven children settled in Saanich.

Their first home was an abandoned 14-by-20-foot log cabin; cracks in the roof were sealed with moss and the floor was made of rough lumber. A few years later they built a larger home, without moss, near the intersection of today's West Saanich Road and Sluggett Avenue.

By the time of John's death, the Sluggett estate was nearly 1,100 acres. Whenever he saw a piece of land going for a good price, he would mortgage everything to get it. As his grandson Lorne Thomson said, "You had to be careful – he'd skin you quicker than you could say 1,000 acres." He was one farm short of owning contiguous parcels stretching from one side of the peninsula to the other.

Fanny Sluggett's butter, eggs and legendary Devonshire cream paid for much of the land and fed the family. She used to make between 30 and

40 pounds of butter per week and collected 20 to 30 dozen eggs. She sold to neighbours and drove into Victoria once a week to sell extra produce.

Though John was undoubtedly shrewd and driven by business interests, he provided numerous community services. He operated one of the first post offices, and his wife served as postmistress. John Sluggett and George Stelly donated one acre each for the West Saanich School in 1880, the first public school in the area. John was also instrumental in the Church community: he helped establish the Calvary Baptist Church in Victoria and organized a Sunday school and church at Shady Creek. Community spirit seemed to be in the genes, because John's children helped build the Sluggett Memorial Church in honour of their parents in 1911. The church was erected with volunteer labour consisting mainly of family members.

John was briefly involved in local politics when he opposed the Island Settlement Act. The Act proposed to give the Dunsmuir Coal Company a large slice of the Island with a cash grant of $750,000 for building a railway from Esquimalt to Nanaimo. He contested the local riding, but he was defeated and the bill was passed.

Like so many other pioneer farms, the land today bears little resemblance to the original Sluggett house and property. Even the name is different, because R.M. Horne Payne, president of the British Columbia Electric Company, renamed it Brentwood Bay in 1925 after his home in Essex, England.

The Sluggett land was divided among John's seven children when he died, and some of the land remains in the family, farmed by the descendants of the pioneers who built the foundation for this Saanich community.

Mohan Jawl (Courtesy Times Colonist)

Jawl Family – 100 Years in Saanich

MOHAN JAWL

Mohan Jawl

Mohan Jawl remembers, as a child, watching the older East Indian men in Centennial Square who gathered daily to pass the hours sharing the stories of their lives. He remembers thinking, it'd be nice to have a story to tell. While Mohan insists that the collective family story is more important than an individual one, there is no doubt that he does indeed have a story to tell.

For the Jawl family, the importance of the year 1906 has little to do with Saanich's incorporation as a municipality. 1906 is the start of the family's history in Canada. In the early 1900s, the lime quarry operating at the future Butchart Gardens recruited workers from communities in India. Mohan's grandfather made the journey to Vancouver Island, where he lived out by the quarry with other employees there. Mohan's father moved to Canada in 1925, returning to India to bring his young wife over in 1930. The couple settled in Saanich, where they raised their four sons: Karnel, Sohan, Robert and Mohan, and two daughters, Jeto and Puge, (a third daughter passed away in childhood). As their family grew, the Jawls lived in homes on Harriet Road, Cloverdale and Douglas Street.

Growing up in Saanich, Mohan attended Tolmie School, S.J. Willis Junior Secondary School and Mount View High School, where his six older siblings had been students before him. After school and during the summer holidays he worked for the family business, driving trucks or selling firewood. At the time, Jawl Industries, formed in 1964, was primarily a building supply enterprise, though its focus would change as the business flourished and expanded. In 1972, the head office of Jawl Industries and its Home Lumber and Building Supplies was at 470 Ardersier Road, in a building designed by Arthur Erickson, one of Canada's leading contemporary architects.

After high school Mohan attended Victoria College for two years before transferring to the University of British Columbia in Vancouver to complete a Bachelor of Commerce degree. In 1968, he finished at the top of his graduating class, and was awarded a coveted Commonwealth Scholarship to further his studies overseas. His trip to the United Kingdom was the first time Mohan had travelled outside British Columbia. He completed his degree at the London School of Economics, then faced the difficult decision of whether to return to Canada, or pursue a legal career in a new city. A sense of family duty brought him home, and after clerking for two judges on the Supreme Court of Canada, Mohan took his place in the family business which had expanded during his years away.

In 1973, Jawl Industries had purchased Cordova Bay Golf Course and the surrounding area—400 acres south of Mattick's farm—which included Lochside Park. With the work of dedicated volunteers, the park became an important part of the community where soccer and baseball leagues play, and walkers enjoy the Lochside Regional Trail. After years of leasing the park to Saanich for $1 per annum, the Jawls donated the land to the municipality. The family purchased the Sayward Gravel Pit, which they developed into a sunny 9-hole golf course called The Ridge that opened in June, 1999. Attractive houses, condominiums and open space fill out the property—quite a transformation from ten years before.

Saanich isn't the only community to benefit from Mohan's passion for making better use of public space. He chairs the Downtown Victoria Community Alliance which raises money and develops ideas towards creating a safer and cleaner downtown. At conferences held in November, 2003 and March, 2004, members of the community met with experts from around the world to put forth their vision for downtown in 2020.

"Having had the conference, and getting people energized and organized was timely," he said, "because Victoria is still a wonderful place to live."

That goes for Saanich too. Looking out the windows in Mohan's comfortable office at the Cordova Bay Golf Course, the grass is green and neatly trimmed. The residents and golfers strolling towards the course or their nearby homes look relaxed, enjoying the mild summer weather. Who would want to be anywhere else, he muses. There's a lady who resides on the third floor of the building behind him, he says, who could live anywhere and in whatever style she desires. She chooses Saanich. Mohan agrees with that decision.

"I could never conceive of moving from here," he says, "I love it."

The Helmcken/McTavish Connection

GEORGE MCTAVISH

George Archibald McTavish: 1856 -
Catherine Amelia McTavish: 1855 – 1922

Duncan McTavish: 1882 – 1967
Emilie Craig McTavish: 1888 – 1984

John Sebastion Helmcken: 1824 – 1920
Cecilia Douglas Helmcken: d.1865

When Dr. J.S. Helmcken sailed from London to Vancouver Island in 1850 to become Fort Victoria's first physician and surgeon, a smallpox epidemic broke out on the ship. Helmcken isolated the sick and was scrupulous about disinfecting, so that only one patient of the 80 people on board died of the disease.

Helmcken was a doctor, a father of confederation and a landowner – at one point he owned most of what is now central View Royal. He saw Victoria's transformation from a Fort to a thriving city, and Saanich from a forested wilderness to an independent municipality of farms and settlements.

Helmcken married Cecila, Governor James Douglas' oldest daughter, in 1852. They lived in Helmcken House, the building that stands as a museum near the ParliamentBuildingstoday. They had seven children, one of whom – Catherine Amelia – became George McTavish's wife in 1877.

George (Archie) McTavish was born in New York in 1856. He came to Vancouver Island in 1873 and he and Catherine settled on 640 acres in North Saanich in the area known as Ardmore today. They named their land Invertavish Farm, and they were the first people in the region to install a telephone. Since there were no schools nearby, a private teacher drove to their house every day in a horse and buggy to tutor the children.

Archie was a dedicated horticulturalist, and is usually credited with owning the first nursery in the district. He imported ornamental trees and orchard stock, and two of his black walnut trees are designated as heritage trees. His specialty was petunia seeds, which he marketed in both the United States and Britain. He was also a founding member of the Victoria Yacht Club.

Five Helmcken Daughters in 1906 (Saanich Archives 1981-19-80a)

In 1889, the family moved to Victoria and made their home on Heywood Avenue. Archie built several successful greenhouses. The greenhouses collapsed in the 1916 snowstorm, creating piles of shiny broken glass that crowds of children played on, until parents became so frustrated at the damage to their shoes that the glass was removed.

Archie and Catherine's son, Duncan, married Emilie Craig in Prince Rupert in 1911. In 1949 they moved to 275 Plowright Avenue on land they inherited from Duncan's grandfather, J.S. Helmcken.

Duncan followed in his father's horticulturalist footsteps and served as president and secretary for the Victoria Horticultural Society and president of the View Royal Garden Club. He also received a Centennial Pioneer Medallion to honour pioneers of the district who were born in Canada prior to 1892.

***

The McTavish Family at Mt. Newton Cross Road, c1907
(Saanich Archives 1981-19-93)

Emily Carr seemed unimpressed by Helmcken's medical skills, and had this to say about the doctor: "He took you over to a very dirty uncurtained window, jerked up the blind, and said: 'tongue!' Then he poked you around the middle... He put a wooden trumpet bang down on your chest and stuck his ear to the other end. After listening and grunting he went into the bottle room, took a bottle, blew the dust off it and emptied out the dead flies. Then he went to the shelves and filled it from several other bottles, corked it, gave it to mother, and sent you home to get well on it." She also maintained that people loved him and referred to him as "Dr. Heal-My-Skin" for Helmcken.)

The medical profession has changed since Helmcken's day, but Helmcken and McTavish Roads serve as subtle reminders of an earlier time, when land was $5 an acre, telephones were scarce, and dead insects made regular appearances in the local doctor's pharmacy.

Building of Shelbourne Street through the Tod Farm, c1915
(Saanich Archives 1980-7-2)

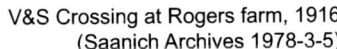

V&S Crossing at Rogers farm, 1916
(Saanich Archives 1978-3-5)

1916 - 1925

In February, 1916, there was a record snowfall—seventy inches in seven days! In that year, municipal services were established to serve the needs of the growing population; hydro lines were installed along East Saanich Road, and water mains installed along Burnside, Wilkinson, Hastings, Holland, Salsbury, Camrose, Ocean View, McRae, Lodge, Falmouth, and the newly constructed Shelbourne Street. A strategic agreement between Saanich and Victoria for extra funding passed when Victoria acknowledged the benefits its residents would gain from access to Saanich parks. The Victoria-Saanich Beaches and Parks Management by-law of 1917 gave the regions joint finance and management of parks in Saanich, and five parks were significantly improved: Cadboro Bay, Mount Douglas, Cordova Bay and Island View in 1917, and Elk Lake in 1922. Services continued to improve with the opening of No. 1 Firehall on Douglas Street in 1917 and the formation of a volunteer fire department in 1919, (a professional fire department superseded this in 1931); and the building of the Saanich War Memorial Health Centre at 4353 West Saanich Road, from which Canada's early public health nurses operated. The Dominion Astrophysical Observatory was completed in 1918, where astronomer John Plaskett's 72-inch telescope—the largest in the world at that time—was housed.

The Grand Old Man of Saanich

FRANK HOBBS

Eliza and Frank Hobbs (Saanich Archives 1980-18-3)

Frank Victor Hobbs: 1862 - 1959
Eliza Hobbs: 1866 - 1958

Ninety-six year old Frank Hobbs attributed his longevity to "keeping active." The farmer, postmaster, businessman, justice of the peace, gardener and school trustee was one of the most active people in Saanich. Even after he retired, Hobbs was a determined and dedicated contributor to the community.

Frank and his brother Edwin moved to Can-

ada from England in 1888. While Edwin settled in Cadboro Bay and started a dairy farm, Frank moved to Port Renfrew to work on the telegraph line. Frank bought a 160-acre piece of property that would later become the "Extension Mine" – an extremely profitable coal mine. But the surrounding lands were owned by the Dunsmuirs, who made it impossible for him to mine the land. After a four-year court battle, Frank sold the land for only $25,000.

Frank stayed in Nanaimo until his brother

tragically died in a farm accident, then moved to Cadboro Bay to help on the family farm, where he worked for several years before selling it and buying land on Sinclair Road.

Frank had grown up in Somerset, England, along with his childhood sweetheart, Eliza. Eliza followed Frank to Canada in 1895 and they married the same year. At the time he was working in the furniture industry, but after 12 years he retired. Believing it was better for his family (Frank and Eliza had a daughter, Francis), Frank and Eliza went back to England – but fortunately for Saanich, they didn't stay. A year later they came back to Canada, and finally, in 1906, settled in Saanich.

In 1906, Cadboro Bay looked much different from today. There were only a few shops: Spencer's Store, Angus Campbell's Ladies Wear, and Morris' Tobacco Store, and by 1914 there was also Frank's grocery store.

Frank worked first as a fruit farmer and then bought the grocery store. Shortly after, he added a post office, and he worked as postmaster for nearly thirty years. The big snow storm of 1916 made his store a vital addition to the community: the storm was so severe that citizens couldn't go into Victoria for supplies, and Frank had to ration food so everyone would have enough.

But perhaps Frank's most significant contribution to the community was served through the school board. He was a school trustee for 14 years, and his goal was to create a high school for Saanich. Finally, with the help of the Minister of Education, the Mount View, Mount Douglas and Mount Newton High schools were built and established. Today, an elementary school is named after him.

He served as a justice of the peace for nearly 50 years and was a member of the Saanich council for two years. Hobbs' commitment to the community was tireless, and in their home at 3830 Hobbs Road (named after his brother Edwin), Frank and Eliza celebrated their 60th wedding anniversary and lived to enjoy their five grandchildren and two great-grandchildren.

View down Sinclair's Hill to Cadboro Bay, early 1900's (Saanich Archives 1980-18-1)

From Dairy Cows to Golf Balls

THE McRAE FAMILY

George McRae: d.1901
Elizabeth Kelly: 1865 -

If you've ever golfed at Cedar Hill Golf Course or walked through the 13-acre park, or used the Cedar Hill Recreation Centre's indoor tennis courts, you may have noticed that the property is an island of green space in a sea of suburbia. You may have even wondered why.

The land on which people sink their putts

Kate and Jean McRae (Saanich Archives 1980-13-3)

and hit their drives on today used to grow wheat and feed cattle. In 1886, the McRae family bought the 150-acre farm from the Hudson's Bay Company and they continued to farm it until 1950, preserving the land from the development occurring in the surrounding areas.

George McRae was born in Dunedin, New Zealand, in the early 1860's. His wife, Elizabeth Kelley, was born in 1865 in California. They met in Seattle, Washington and married in 1886, and shortly after established their farm in Saanich. They had five children; the eldest of whom, Katherine McRae, became the first public health nurse in Saanich.

George died in 1901, a year before their house at 1445 Ocean View was completed. Elizabeth McRae was left with five children and over 100 cows to look after, and she probably wanted to return to her family in the United States (after her husband died, she reportedly kept a shotgun close by.) But each time she tried to sell the property, the deal did not go through and it reverted to her. So, it is almost by default that this piece of property was preserved for the municipality's use.

She first rented 60 acres of the property for a golf course in 1917, while the rest of the land continued to serve as a farm. It wasn't until 1967 that the Saanich municipality expropriated the McRae estate for the cost of $1.2 million, updated the golf course and built the Recreation Centre.

The Cedar Hill Community Centre was officially opened on May 1, 1973, at 3220 Cedar Hill Road, along with a 13-acre park. They continue to make improvements to the Centre and the golf course to accommodate Saanich's increasing population and needs. Today the former McRae estate is an important green area and recreational space in the midst of urban development.

The McRae family home that George started to build over a hundred years ago still stands at 1445 Ocean View Road. Now it serves as the Saanich Volunteer Services Society's headquarters, a non-profit agency that provides services such as volunteer driving, dog walking and minor home repairs to seniors and other residents of Saanich. It sits on the 18th hole of the golf course, and the view – from dairy cows and wheat, to fairways and golf balls – a little different today.

The McRae Farmhouse in 1925 (Saanich Archives 1980-13-2)

This biography has been sponsored by

575 Gorge Road East, Victoria, BC V8T 2W5
Phone: (250) 386-7586 Fax: (250) 386-4550

Plaskett's Window to the Heavens

JOHN PLASKETT

(Courtesy Dominion Astrophysical Observatory)

Dr. John Stanley Plaskett C.B.E.: 1865 – 1941
Rebecca Plaskett

"From that hill in Saanich, John Plaskett made the greatest single contribution to Canadian astronomy – the discovery of the principle of galactic rotation, a means to determine the distance of the sun from the centre of the galaxy."

From a distance, it looks like a giant white pencil eraser, jutting out of the trees like Alice in Wonderland after she ate that tiny piece of cake. Up close, The Dominion Astrophysical Observatory on Little Saanich Mountain is an impressive structure. The dome is 75 feet high, and consists of double-steel wall construction. The telescope's original glass mirror was 72 inches in diameter, 13 inches thick and weighed approximately 4,500 pounds. When it was completed in 1918, it was the largest telescope in the world.

As the telescope brought the stars a little closer to earth, it put Canada in the forefront of stellar research. The Observatory was the result of one man's persistence and careful research; a man who, though he dropped out of high school to work on his family's farm, became Canada's greatest astronomer.

John Plaskett was born in 1865 in Hickson, Ontario, and left school when he was 16. He became a mechanic, and began working in the University of Toronto's physics department when he was 24. With his wife Rebecca's support, he began studying engineering part time and graduated at age 34 with a degree and first-class honours in physics and mathematics.

By 1903, John was working for the observatory branch in Ottawa, which had only a 15-inch refractor telescope. He continually lobbied parliament to build a larger instrument, and in 1913, he was finally granted funds for a 72-inch telescope.

There were several sites investigated for the new Observatory, including Penticton and Ottawa, but the Saanich site was eventually chosen for its mild weather and short distance from town. As it was just a short distance off West Saanich Road, it was far enough away from town that the lights wouldn't interfere with star-gazing.

Plaskett was director of the Observatory from 1918 until he retired in 1935, and he made the Observatory, and its home, famous. In 1922 he discovered a double star, now named Plaskett's Twins, that remained the heaviest star on record for many years. In 1967, a crater on the moon was named for him. He was also the first Canadian astronomer to become a Fellow of the Royal Society.

Although the telescope was built almost a century ago, it has been modernized and is still in use. The Observatory would no doubt make its founder proud: it continues to inform and entertain visitors, and its astronomers have made various discoveries over the years that have kept it within the scope of the scientific community.

In 2001, the National Research Council of Canada expanded the Observatory and opened an astronomy interpretative centre called the Centre of the Universe. The $2 million, 7,000 square-foot addition was the first of its kind in Canada. It introduces visitors to the complex and fascinating field of astronomy, where they can not only

Dr Plaskett with the completed telescope
(Saanich Archives 1993-1-19)

see comets and Saturn's rings, but they can learn about them and about Canada's contributors to the field of astronomy – including one man whose vision and talent created an invaluable and lasting Saanich landmark.

Rudd Park (Saanich Archives)

Hard Work, Persistence, and Reward
MARTHA RUDD

Martha Newton Starkey Rudd: 1850 - 1928

In the early 20th century, land in Saanich was abundant and cheap. With a small amount of savings, it was possible to buy a few acres and start a farm. However, there were many people who arrived in Canada with neither money nor skills. While many thought they would get lucky on a gold strike, getting rich that way was a rarity, and buying uncleared land with the intention of forming a farm and making a profit from it was perhaps as big a gamble as panning for gold.

But Martha Rudd, a single mother who paid for her land with money she made scrubbing the floor of the local church and cleaning houses, managed to save enough money to buy a few acres on which she created a self-sustaining dairy farm. Despite an abusive husband and a life punctuated by misfortune, she eventually had her dream house. She spent the latter half of her life surrounded by gardens, orchards, and the friendly mooing of a herd of cows that were named after her grandchildren.

Rudd had a well-travelled life before she settled in Saanich (in fact, she didn't arrive in Saanich until she was 50.) In 1876, Rudd immigrated to Australia from England with her husband John. She was 26 years old. For eight years, she worked at odd jobs, without much improvement in the family's circumstances. After her son died, Rudd gave up on Australia and moved to California. California, however, also proved to be a disappointment, so the Rudd family packed their bags again and migrated to the Gulf Islands.

By the time the Rudd family settled in Victoria in 1900, Martha was 50 and had eight children. She was responsible for raising the children and providing the income; her husband was unreliable and never brought home a steady income. So when he said he wanted to return to England, Martha refused to go. Left to her own devices in Canada, Martha's situation finally began to improve.

After eight years of cleaning houses, she had saved up enough money to buy a plot of land along Burnside Road East. She bought a herd of cows, and with help from the Department of Agriculture, she built Victoria's first grain silo. Her sons built her a house, which she called "Buena Vista," and for 20 years, she lived on the property and ran the dairy farm and a garden.

In 1928, Rudd died and left part of her land to her son Fred, who continued to run the dairy farm until he died at age 75. At the time of his death, his herd was a major milk producer on Vancouver Island.

Martha also left some land to her son George. George Rudd served as a Saanich alderman and was on the Saanich Parks and Recreation Committee. When he died, he donated five acres for parkland to Saanich. Rudd Park offers playground equipment and sports fields, and can be accessed from Irma Street. It has offered joy and entertainment to neighbourhood children since 1943, and largely thanks to the hard work and persistence of a remarkable pioneer.

From Pop Stand to Popular Resort

GEORGE McMORRAN

George McMorran: 1888 - 1971
Ida McMorran: d.1988

McMorran's Beach House, with its popular Charters Restaurant and Sandbar Patio, has long been a popular destination for tourists and locals. Over the years, McMorran's has provided a venue for hundreds of weddings, dances, and banquets. While it is now a thriving business, McMorran's had humble beginnings. It began in 1919 when George McMorran returned from the war and didn't know what to do with himself. His real estate business had been dissolved before the war began, he wasn't a farmer, and Cordova Bay only offered seasonal employment opportunities.

So on May 19th, 1919, he decided he would open an ice cream parlour and pop stand. He barely slept for three days in order to have it built for the May long weekend, but by the 24th the building was open and ready for business. On that first day, he made $4.98.

George was two years old when he first came to Vancouver Island from Paisley, Ontario. His father became the manager of the 1,000-acre Rithet Farm in Royal Oak. Among other things, his father was responsible for clearing the land, and, as this was long before dynamite was used to remove stumps, blasting powder was used instead.

In 1900, the family moved to a 12-acre home on Cedar Hill Road. Though the family never lived in Cordova Bay, they would vacation there every summer. George had fond memories of "living shoeless" and playing on the beach.

In 1909, he joined forces with another pio-

The McMorran Family (Saanich Archives 1980-20-1)

neer to form Dougall and McMorran, a real estate company. They were responsible for some early subdivision of Doumac Avenue in Cordova Bay. A few years later, the real estate business crashed, the company was dissolved, and George went to war. From 1914 to 1918, George served as a gunner in World War I. After he got back, he was at loose ends. Then, a friend suggested to him that he open a store.

So in 1919, he opened a one-room, six-foot-by-12-foot ice cream parlour. Two years later, he built a larger building on the property next door and called it McMorran's Tea Rooms, which became the location of the renowned Saturday night dances. In fact, McMorran's dances became so well known that in 1989, CBC television came to film a dance because the producer was "convinced she had found something special."

In 1923, George married Ida Richards, a schoolteacher who occasionally would help him in the store, when she wasn't teaching at the Bank Street School. They had four children: Eric, Bruce, Richard and David. When George retired, his sons Eric and Bruce became managers and updated and expanded the resort.

In 1926, George became the first postmaster for the region and installed gas pumps and operated an auto camp. He was responsible for bringing most of the utilities and services to Cordova Bay, including the set up of a pipe system to a local spring to provide drinking water (the pipe system is still in use today.)

Today, McMorran's Beach House provides a venue for musicians, comedians, and even young performers. It has remained a family owned and operated business for over 80 years. When George McMorran pulled together the lumber to build his single-room operation, he probably little realized that it would become Cordova Bay's most sought-after locale.

Mr McMorran (left) blasting a stump on Broadmead Farm (Saanich Archives 1980-20-4)

This biography has been sponsored by

49

From Limestone to Lillies:
The Butchart Gardens
THE BUTCHART FAMILY

Jennie Butchart: 1866 - 1950
Robert Butchart: 1856 – 1943

When Jennie Butchart stood at the edge of the Tod Inlet limestone quarry, she saw acres of scarred grey rock, inhospitable to anything green and growing. Though the cement factory had given her and her husband the means to build a mansion and become one of the few families on Vancouver Island to own a car, it had turned the back yard of her Saanich home into an unsightly pit.

In an effort to disguise the ugliness of the pit, Jennie planted sweet peas and white poplars in between the house and the quarry. As the quarry ran out of limestone, she continued to extend the garden, eventually moving topsoil and planting flowers directly in the pit itself. Through her efforts and her husband's support, one of Victoria's most celebrated tourist attractions, the Butchart Gardens, was born.

Robert (Bob) Butchart first began manufacturing Portland cement in 1888 in Ontario. He

Mr and Mrs Butchart, c1940
(Courtesy of The Butchart Gardens Ltd)

saw potential in the rich limestone deposits on the west coast, and by 1904, the Butcharts had established their home near the new factory in Tod Inlet. The west coast was exploding with development, and concrete was in great demand to build roads, buildings and railways. The Butchart company put Victoria on the map as a provincial innovator in concrete highway construction, and Bob was called "the father of the Canadian cement industry." But by 1921 the Tod Inlet pit had completely run out of limestone, leaving a huge excavation for Jeannie to turn into a world-renowned tourist attraction. Bob supported his wife whole-heartedly in her venture, reportedly supplying whatever was necessary to repair the grey pit, and spared workers from the factory to work on the gardens.

The result is 55 acres of riotous colour and exotic plants. The Butcharts, who had a penchant for travel, planted more than 5,000 varieties of plants collected from all over the world, including places as far-flung as the Himalayas and the Pyrenees. With its Italian, Japanese and English rose gardens, the Butchart Gardens brings an international flavour to the area.

One hundred years later, the Gardens are still owned by the Butchart family. In 1939, Jennie and Bob Butchart passed them on to their grandson, Robert Ian Ross. After the war, the gardens were running a deficit of up to $20,000 a year, and Ross had a choice: continue running them, or subdivide. He chose to keep the gardens.

The Butcharts called their estate "Benvenuto," which is the Italian word for welcome, and today the gardens welcome about 1.3 million people every year, with as many as 10,000 appearing on Saturday nights to view the fireworks. It employs up to 600 people during the high season and 250 full-time employees. It has created a huge tourism draw and bolstered an economy that is almost entirely dependent on tourism.

The only thing left to remind people that this vibrant collage of colour and life was once a cement factory is a single chimney from a forgotten kiln, visible only from the lookout point in the sunken garden. Though the Butcharts could have left the scar of a quarry on the landscape forever, they created a legacy that has been en-

Mrs Butchart, c1910 (Courtesy of The Butchart Gardens Ltd)

joyed through the last century, and will continue to be enjoyed through the next.

Wright Everytime
STAN V. WRIGHT

Stanley Victor Wright: 1906 – 2001

Behind the rows of magazines, the piles of newspapers and the racks of romance novels at Thrifty Foods, BC ferries and other newsstands throughout Vancouver Island, is the story of a certain type of pioneer. Stanley Victor Wright began his career in magazine and news-paper distribution when he was 16 and delivered newspapers on a bicycle. From this arose Stan V. Wright Ltd., a nationally recognized business that supplied publications to locations throughout Vancouver Island for 75 years.

The business was founded in 1922 by Harold Lovick, who named it Lovick's News Agency. While Wright took over the business not long after it was founded, he didn't rename it Stan V. Wright Ltd. until it was moved to its Quadra street location in 1962. Operated by Wright, and later by his wife and sons, the successful company was a reg-ular employer in Victoria and Saanich for decades. They also operated Yates News and Books, a newsstand that operated at Yates Street for 12 years before it was closed in 1997.

Stan V. Wright in December 2000
(Courtesy Vicki Sanders)

Wright was an avid athlete, a dedicated family man and a successful business owner. He was a member of the United Commercial Travellers (UTC) and the Elks. Known to never miss reading several daily newspapers, he lived in Saanich for many of his 95 years. He was born on December 8, 1906, at the Work Point Barracks in Esquimalt, and graduated from Esquimalt High School. His parents, Captain F.R. and Kathleen Wright, raised their children at Signal Hill, an environment that fostered Wright's passion for the sea. When they retired, they moved to Gladstone Avenue. An avid athlete, Wright played soccer for Esquimalt, Oaklands, Vic West, the Hudson's Bay and others; he played lacrosse for Lampson Street, Esquimalt, Sidney, Garrison and Foundation; he played tennis and badminton at Hillcrest, C.P.R. and Kingston Street.

In 1931, Wright married Margaret Wilson, and they would enjoy a 61-year marriage until Margaret died in 1992. In 1958, the Wrights had moved to a three-acre property on 1230 Reynolds Road, where Wright lived un-til he passed away in 2001. Their second home was called "Hahlakl," which means wide open spaces. Situated on Kaltasin Road in Sooke, Stan and Margaret built the house together in 1942. They used it for a summer retreat, and Wright spent many of his early retirement years there boating, fishing and salvaging logs.

During his career, he held the position of secretary treasurer for both the Western Canadian Independent Wholesalers and the Periodical Distributors of Canada; the latter named him "Wholesaler of the Year" in 1954 and 1955. For five consecutive years, SM News named him the top Canadian wholesaler.

After Wright retired, the business continued to operate at its final location, 2120 Quadra Street, under the ownership of his sons. It was sold in 1997 to Pacific Periodicals of Vancouver.

The industry was becoming increasingly consolidated into fewer – but larger – distribution agencies. In 1995, there were 350 in Canada and the U.S., and two years later, only 80.

When he passed away at age 95, Wright was survived by two daughters (Jo-Anne Gurney and Vicki Sanders) three sons (Fred, Loran and Wayne), 12 grandchildren and 17 great-grandchildren. Nicknamed "The Candy Man" for the profusion of candies that he always kept handy in his home, he was a beloved father and grandfather.

As an employer, an athlete and a volunteer, Stan Wright led a productive and distinguished life. He kept the shelves stocked with reading material, and cultivated many friendships along the way.

(Courtesy Vicki Sanders)

Entrepreneur Extraordinaire
ROBERT RITHET

Robert Paterson Rithet: 1844 -1919

Tourism Victoria's headquarters at 1117 Wharf Street was built over a century ago, but thanks to a 1977 renovation, the building looks almost identical to how it did when it belonged to businessman Robert Rithet. Rithet, a former Victoria mayor, member of the legislative assembly and Saanich resident, originally used the building for his wholesale business in 1871. Now, "Rithet's Block" is a monument to the man who had the drive and motivation to turn Victoria into the bustling tourist attraction it is today.

It was 1862 and Rithet was 18 years old when he left Scotland and came to British Columbia to join the gold rush in the Cariboo. Within two years he left, because he realized he preferred business to panning for gold. He moved to California where he met Andrew Welch, who was laying the foundations of a sugar refining business.

Rithet became increasingly involved with Welch & Company, until in 1871 he expanded the business to Vancouver Island and the company became known as Welch, Rithet & Company. Splitting his time between Vancouver Island and San Francisco allowed Rithet to develop his Victoria businesses and Saanich farms, while Welch, Rithet and Company became a leader in the cane sugar industry in Hawaii and along the Pacific Coast. When Welch died in 1888, the company was renamed R.P. Rithet & Co Ltd. The firm imported groceries, liquor and sugar into North America.

In 1875, Rithet married Elizabeth Munro, the

(Courtesy BC Archives A-1734)

daughter of a Hudson's Bay employee. They had three children, and built their house "Hollybank" at 952 Humboldt Street.

Rithet owned a vast amount of land in Saanich, including the 1,000-acre Broadmead

Farm where he raised racehorses (he named the farm after his favourite horse, Broadmead.) He was one of the first people on Vancouver Island to clear and farm the heavily forested land in that area. Included in Rithet's landholdings was Rithet's Bog, a particularly important area today because it is the last intact peat bog remaining in the Greater Victoria area.

Rithet kept his hand in many business interests, including groceries, insurance, shipping, brokerage and railways; he was also involved in a failed venture that attempted to lay a telegraph cable across the Pacific. When ill health forced him to retire, the family settled permanently in Victoria.

Rithet became mayor of Victoria in 1885 and a member of the legislative assembly from 1894 to 1898. He also played a pivotal role in the construction of the outer harbour of Victoria, known as "Rithet's folly." Later, it was lauded as playing a vital part in Vancouver Island's development, because the outer harbour could accommodate the large deep-sea vessels that the inner harbour could not. It created new trade and commerce opportunities. Rithet's shipping company brought cargoes from all over the world into Victoria.

As the Colonist reported in 1949, "In Victoria, Mr. Rithet took a prominent place both as a businessman and as a public spirited citizen." His determination to undertake projects largely unaided and in the face of criticism has also helped create the municipality of Saanich as we know it today.

Broadmead Farm, c1893 (Saanich Archives 1980-20-6)

The Adventurous Bordens

THE BORDEN FAMILY

Frank Nobel Borden: 1859 - 1933
Millie (Pickard) Borden: 1869 - ?
Fred Borden: 1898 - 1996
Charles Borden: 1902 - 1994

The Borden family originated in New England, but around 1760 part of the family left the States and settled in Nova Scotia. Three Nova Scotia Bordens, born in the late 19th century, went on to become some of the most influential Canadians in history.

There was Sir Robert Borden, Prime Minister of Canada from 1911 to 1920, and Dr. Lorris Elijah Borden, the last surviving member of the "lost expedition" to the Arctic in 1903 who died in Victoria in 1963. But for Saanich residents, no Borden has been more influential to the community than Frank Nobel Borden.

Frank grew up in Nova Scotia and didn't come to Victoria until he was 31. He originally worked as a builder, but after a few years of that he turned to farming, and in 1895 leased the 450-acre property called North Dairy Farm from the Hudson's Bay Company. He cleared the land, planted fruit trees and stocked purebred dairy cattle, sending

Frank Borden, 1916 (Saanich Archives)

the cream to the old Victoria Dairy on Douglas Street.

The beginning of Frank's farming career corresponded with his marriage; in 1895, he married Millie, a schoolteacher in the two-room schoolhouse at Cadboro Bay (now the site of the Uplands Golf Course.) Their first son, Edgar, was born in 1896; Fred was born in 1898; their only daughter Winifred was born in 1900; and Charles was born in 1902.

Frank demonstrated a steady and preserving commitment to the community in his 74 years. He served on the Saanich council from 1910-1916 and served as Reeve from 1917 and 1918.

His son Fred followed in Frank's footsteps in many respects, and at age 28 was sworn in as a freshman member of council. At the time, municipal politics were a little different from what they are today; for instance, council members were elected every year instead of every three years. When Borden was elected in 1927, the entire Saanich election budget totaled only $507.08. The population was 12,000 people, and that included Ward

6, which later became the present municipality of Central Saanich.

However, Fred didn't share his father's passion for farming, and said that the only brother who did was Edgar, who died in 1920 in a farming accident. Thus, when Frank Borden died in 1933, Fred recognized that the demands of the family farm superseded his desire to work as a civil engineer. He ran the farm for 13 years until 1946, when the poor price of milk and the difficulties in hiring workers forced him to sell the farm.

So Fred moved to Blenkinsop Road and opened a garage at the corner of Quadra and Reynolds. His brother Charles also opened a feed and grain store called the Borden Mercantile Co. on Quadra Street, property that was once part of the old farm. The business is still in operation today.

Although the farm and the Borden land are now unrecognizable, the family remained a presence in the municipality of Saanich from the day it was incorporated until well into the 20th century.

Fred Borden, 1927 (Saanich Archives)

This biography has been sponsored by

Grand opening of the first Saanich Thrifty Foods location. *Quadra Centre*	Alex Campbell unveils his next Thrifty Foods *Broadmead Village*	Thrifty Foods expands in Saanich yet again. *Quadra at Cloverdale*	The most recent addition to Saanich Thrifty Foods family. *Hillside Shopping Cenre*	Growing in Saanich *Tuscany Village*
1980	**1991**	**1997**	**2000**	**2006**

Proudly Serving Saanich Communities Since 1980   **THRIFTY** FOODS™

The Functional, Elegant Architect
HUBERT SAVAGE

Hubert Savage: 1885 – 1955

Hubert Savage was a well-known architect who designed many of the Arts and Crafts style buildings that exist today in Victoria and Saanich. His list of commissions include Mount View High School (which became a Camosun College campus) and the Royal Oak Inn (later the home of the Maltwood Museum, and now a restaurant.) Though he died in 1955, many of his buildings still exist, and many have become designated heritage houses.

Savage was born in London, England, in 1885. He was educated at Hilmartin College in St. Albans, and articled with a firm of London architects and attended the Regent Street Polytechnic before he immigrated to Canada in 1912. He made a successful career in Canada, and became so well known that when one of his houses is up for sale, real estate agents still advertise it as a Savage design.

The Arts and Crafts movement had a great influence on architecture in North America between 1880-1920. This type of

(City of Victoria Archives PR73-6024)

architecture was very different from high Victorian architecture. Informal and unpretentious, the goal of Arts and Crafts architecture was simple, functional elegance that complemented the environment. The two leading architects of the day were Francis Rattenbury and Samuel Maclure; the former, who designed the Empress Hotel and the parliament buildings, established himself as the foremost designer of institutions, while Maclure focused on residential homes.

Savage worked with both Maclure and Percy Leonard James. He took over the work that was incomplete when Maclure died in 1929, and he worked in partnership with James until 1951. Most of Savage's homes are typical of the Cotswold cottage design, with a garden setting, simple wrought iron hardware for doors and windows, and heavy half-beams in the ceiling.

Savage designed his own home in 1914 on Blackwood Road, which would later become Grange road (ex-Saanich Councillor, and current MLA David Cubberly, now lives in the house.) Savage lived there for over 40 years with his wife, Alys, and their daughter. The Savage house has cross-gables and a large entrance porch, supported by three posts that stand on sloping-sided stone piers.

Possibly Savage's best known work is the 1939 Arts and Crafts style "cottage," originally known as the Royal Oak Inn, later as UVic's Maltwood Museum, and later still as the Chantecler restaurant and the Fireside Grill. When Mr. and Mrs. Forrest commissioned the building in 1939, they wanted to start a restaurant. The dining hall was 30 by 50 feet, was 25-feet high and had stone fireplaces at either end. Savage included a gallery that overlooked the hall for the musicians. Unfortunately for the Forrests, the onset of the war made it financially impossible to run a restaurant, and they were forced to sell in 1941.

Savage designed the only designated heritage house in Sidney. Built in 1937 and currently belonging to Cyril Hume, the arched shape to the entrance and the weatherboard in the gables is indicative of the English Arts and Crafts style; one person described it as resembling a teapot. The house also has diamond-shaped, leaded glass windows, another design element Savage used frequently.

This house was originally built for a Ms. Stuart, and rumour says she was looking for a retirement home for herself and a "romantic attachment". After the house's completion, the "attachment" didn't work out, and Ms. Stuart rented the house shortly after. She finally sold the cottage in 1944. The house and the garden have been profiled in Canadian Living, Canadian Gardening, Country Gardens and the Times Colonist. Other houses designed by Savage that are now designated heritage houses include "Hall Cottage" at Knockan Hill Park and "Addendum," on Burnside Road West.

When Savage died in 1955, he had recently been made a life member of the Royal Institute of British Architects. His work reviving the Arts and Crafts style, and designing so many elegant and unobtrusive houses in the community, makes him well deserving of the honour.

Health Nurses and their cars at the Municipal Yard, Douglas
Street, 1934 (Saanich Archives 1980-15-269)

Craigflower School class of 1932
(Saanich Archives 1982-10-3)

1926 - 1935

During prohibition rum running was very profitable. Johnny Schnarr, a Carboro Bay resident made 400 runs and retired before he was forty. Others, like many Canadians, struggled through the Great Depression in the 1930s when little financial relief could be found, sometimes working on roads for twenty cents an hour. One industry that did boom was liquor production, when the Growers Wine Company erected the first portion of the Winery at Lake Hill in 1927. Prior to this, the company had rented an old building on Wharf street where it manufactured Loganberry wine. The move to Saanich meant an increase in product, including blackberry and grape wines, vermouth and brandy. In the coming years however, the cost of importing grapes from as far as the Okanagan Valley, as well as shipping the finished product, led to the sale of the company to one on the mainland. Though the Growers Wine Company is no longer active in Saanich, it was a precursor to the many wineries that flourish on Vancouver Island today.

In 1928, B.C.'s first licensed airport opened at Lansdowne Field. Continued development along Maplewood, Blenkinsop, Wilkinson, West Saanich Road and at Elk Lake was matched by new municipal services. Telephone lines were established, and Saanich's first high schools, Mount Douglas, Mount Newton and Mount View, were funded and opened by the municipality, Saanich Council and the School Board in 1931. A year later the first sighting of Cadborosaurus was reported. By 1935 the CN Railway track north of Lakehill was abandoned.

An Old Saanich Cowboy

JOE BULL

Josiah Bull Senior: 1864 - 1939
Ellen Speed: 1871 - 1946
Joe Bull: 1896 - 1965
Gladys Fairclough: 1900 – 1985

In 1930, there were five members on the Saanich Police force, one car, three motorcycles and a push bike. The horses had been sold a few years earlier because of the high cost of oats ($22 a month). There were no vacations, and the officers received only one night and one day off a week – and if there was a special event, even that was forfeit.

Despite these hardships, Josiah Bull Jr. joined the police force on March 1st of 1930. Though a farmer at heart, Bull was evidently good at his job: only eight years after joining, he became Police Chief. By many reports, there could not have been a more effective or diplomatic man for the job.

Bull grew up on his father's 40-acre dairy farm in Royal Oak. He always planned to become a farmer, but perhaps policing was in his blood: his grandfather Thomas Speed had also been an officer, and once nearly died from blood poisoning when a man who was resisting arrest bit him.

Bull's parents, Josiah and Ellen, raised dairy cows at Manor Farm, atop Rithet's Hill on North Quadra Street. The stone house they built at 4201 Quadra Street is a designated heritage house today. They had seven children. One of their daughters, Elizabeth, was the first stenographer to work for the municipality of Saanich.

Joe married Gladys Fairclough in 1926 and they had four children. In 1938 Bull became police chief and the force acquired a second car. In 1941 they had four cars, and a two-way ra-

(Saanich Archives 1992-17-1)

dio. At the end of the World War II the force was enlarged, but it was not until 1950 that the three-shift system was in effect so each person would get an equal amount of time off.

Joe retired from the Saanich Police force in 1957 and returned to the stone house and original five acres of the Bull farm that he and his wife retained.

(Saanich Archives 1981-25-5)

He saw the force transform into its greatly improved situation from rather primitive beginnings. In 1889, the B.C. Provincial Police provided the Saanich Peninsula with one resident constable; the position was later cut to save money. Predictably, the incidence of petty crimes – particularly chicken theft – increased.

In 1906, when hundreds of people petitioned the Lieutenant Governor to make the district a municipality, one of the first things they did was post a job for a Constable/Sanitary Officer who patrolled the 70 square miles of Saanich and Central Saanich on horseback. By 1915, the men wore khaki uniforms and riding breeches, causing the Victoria Police to call them "The Saanich Cowboys." That year the squad bought a car; a $500 Ford they purchased with the proceeds from the sale of a horse and a motorcycle.

Joe Armstrong, the Deputy Police Chief in 1964, once wrote, "Chief Josiah Bull was one of the kindest men that I have ever met. His friends ran the full gamut of humanity from the poorest to the richest, and from the lowest to the highest. In his office you might find a Hindu wood peddler or the Lieutenant Governor and all conditions in between."

This biography has been sponsored by the
SAANICH POLICE DEPARTMENT

Crusader in Petticoats

NELLIE McCLUNG

(Saanich Archives 1981-23-4)

Nellie Letitia McClung: 1873 – 1961

When Nellie McClung lived in Manitoba, she loved to gallop her horse across the open fields of the prairies. One evening she was thrown, but instead of blaming the horse or the uneven ground, she brushed herself off and said it wouldn't have happened if she had been riding astride, the proper way. But the side-saddle was "just another example of life's injustice to women."

Probably Canada's best-known early feminist, McClung has been called a crusader, a "hyena in petticoats," and "one of the most admired, and hated, women in Canada." But to her friends, family and neighbours, Nellie presented a very different side. McClung moved to the Gordon Head area after she retired in 1934. As a delegate to the League of Nations she offered a political window to Saanich residents, as many politicians, writers and actors came to visit her at home on Ferndale Road. She was known for donating massive quantities of flowers and occasionally stepping in to give the Sunday sermon at St. Aidan's Church.

While most famous for fighting for women's rights (including her infamous encounter with Manitoba premier Sir Rodmond Roblin, who told her that that "nice women don't want the vote"), McClung's accomplishments went far beyond her work in the suffragist movement.

McClung was an author who wrote more than 17 books, numerous essays and short stories. While living in Gordon Head, she wrote *Leaves from Lantern Lane* and *The Streams Run Fast*. She called her Saanich home "Lantern Lane" because she always hung a lantern at the end of the lane. The connection to her books made 1861 Ferndale Road a landmark.

The one-and-a-half storey house was built in 1914 by Saanich builder Edward James Merritt for John Fullerton, a second engineer from 1877 to 1878 on the Hudson's Bay Company's steamship Beaver. The Beaver has been called "the ship that saved the West" and, as the first steamship in the region, it played a vital role in the history and development of the West Coast. Like McClung, Fullerton moved to Gordon Head when he retired at age 60.

However, McClung's road to retirement was a long one. After only five years of formal education she worked as a schoolteacher in Manitou at age 16. There, she met her husband, pharmacist Wesley McClung. They raised five children and were happily married for over 50 years.

Many people accused her of neglecting her husband and children for the sake of her political work, but her family was loyal and supportive. One day her son Horace found his younger brother out in front of the house looking very dirty and he hustled him into the house, saying, "Quick! It's a good thing I saw you before the newspapers got a picture of you – Nellie McClung's neglected child!"

When Nellie and Wes moved to Winnipeg in 1911, she became a founding member of The Political Equality League. The group was principally concerned with women's suffrage, but also with other issues such as the appointment of more (female) factory inspection workers, to keep a check on the nefarious sweat shops in Winnipeg.

When Wes was transferred to Alberta, Nellie continued to speak in public and began writing a newspaper column called "Nellie McClung Says." She was on the Alberta Legislature from 1921 to 1926, and in 1929 was part of the "famous five" who went to court to have women declared as legal "persons" who were therefore eligible to vote.

While Nellie McClung may have been a hyena to her political opponents, her Saanich neighbours considered her kind and understanding. Few of them realized the extent of her political influence or the honours she had been given; they simply knew that the McClungs were very generous with homemade sauerkraut and dill pickles. When she died in 1951, the number of people who attended her funeral was so large that the service had to be held in the large Metropolitan Church in the city.

In tribute to her contribution to Canada, Nellie was commemorated on a postage stamp in 1974 and the Nellie McClung Library was opened in 1976. In recognition of its historical significance, "Lantern Lane" at 1861 Ferndale Road was designated a heritage house in 1988.

From Student to Teacher at the University School

REG WENMAN

Reg Wenman: 1903 – 1988

Reg Wenman was the most prolific rungetter in Canadian cricket. During a 40-year career, he scored a record 37 centuries, coming second only to an American player who scored 38. The Victoria Sports Hall of Fame considers him to be not only the most prolific player, but also one of the greatest cricketers in Canadian history.

Yet Wenman isn't best known in Saanich for his athletic ability. His teaching career at the University School on Richmond Road spanned more than 46 years. When his years as a student are included, he was with the University School from almost the beginning of its existence until it amalgamated with St. Michael's in 1971, and became St. Michaels University School.

Wenman lived in Saanich for most of his life, barring the years he served in the war overseas, and the time he spent in the interior recuperating from a three-year bout with tuberculosis. He was born in 1903 in Souris, Manitoba, where his parents, John and Alice, had a homestead. In 1906, the Wenman's moved back to England (Alice couldn't abide the Manitoba farming life) but they moved back to Canada – and to Saanich – in 1912. That year, in the height of the land boom, the Wenman's bought 10 acres in the Gordon Head area for $2,000 an acre. The house is named Acryse, and the exterior looks exactly

as it did when it was first built at 2144 Wenman Drive (the road is named after the family.)

The University School was founded when three men – Reverend William Bolton, James Barnacle and Captain Harvey – amalgamated their three existing private schools into one. In 1908, they purchased 15 acres at the foot of Mt. Tolmie (they wanted plenty of flat land for their sports fields) and on October 7, Premier Richard McBride laid the first corner stone of the building. In February 1909, classes opened on the present-day campus with approximately 80 students registered.

By 1912, when nine-year-old Wenman first began attending the school, there were 137 boarders and 47-day students. As a day student, Wenman managed to avoid the mandatory (and bitterly cold) showers, although it meant he was subject to the teasing of the other children. In one article that he wrote for the school's magazine the Red and Black, he said, "The day boys, of which I was one, were the lowest forms of life."

But despite being a low form of life, Reg became a cricket great through the training he received at the school. He would go on to play cricket for Canada and rugby for the Victoria Reps, and to be inducted into the Victoria Sports Hall of Fame in 1998. He was captain and unofficial star of the cricket team the "Incogs" (the team is composed of people with past or present school connections), and he was a member from about 1920 to 1980.

He married Evelyn Lytton in 1942, and they had three children, all of whom were active in sports. Their daughter Joan was an avid field hockey player, and both of their sons became teachers, and played both cricket and rugby. For a time, he and his family lived on the school property in Harvey House, but in 1951 they moved back into the family home on Wenman Drive.

In 1971, when Wenman retired, former students praised his positive attitude, high standards and commitment to the well being of the pupils. That same year, due to financial difficulties, the University School and St. Michael's amalgamated and became St. Michaels University School. In 1986, the school named its new sports facility the Wenman Pavilion in Reg's honour – an appropriate tribute to the dedicated teacher and sports enthusiast.

Reporter Bill Walker once wrote, "First as a pupil at University School, then a master; at war, and in peace; on the playing field, and as an advisor, Reg Wenman has earned an undeniable measure of esteem."

(Courtesy St. Michaels University School, Archives)

A Great Inventor

BARNEY OLDFIELD

Barney Oldfield

Imagine that you had a house with a spectacular view from the living room, and a less spectacular view at the back of the house, from the bedroom. Now imagine if you could flip a switch and have your house rotate, so that you could see that spectacular view from any room.

That's what Barney Oldfield did when he built his twelve-sided, rotating house at 5321 Old West Saanich Road. Built on a motorized shaft, the house could rotate a complete 360 degrees. When Barney died in 1978, the cupola was still incomplete. His other inventions include a specialized logging truck, bulldozer blades, and a custom-built car he built in 1940 called "The Spirit of Tomorrow."

His father, Horace Oldfield, was only 18 years old when he moved to Vancouver Island in 1895. However, less than a year later, he had acquired three large blocks of land at Prospect Lake, where he kept poultry and planted an orchard. He sold extra produce in town. In 1910 he built a house on his property on Prospect Lake Road. He married Mildred, and they had two sons, Basil (known as Barney) and Brian.

As well as being an inventor, Barney Oldfield was a mechanic and an entrepreneur. He knew a little bit about repairing Model T Fords, and so he built a garage at 5295 West Saanich Road in 1935. He was still just a teenager when he scraped together the $25 down payment on the $150 property by working in the general store for a dollar a day – plus lunch and a 5-cent candy bar

in the afternoon. To build the garage, the cow manure was scraped off the boards of his father's barn and was used to form the 24 by 24-foot structure. He also trucked gravel for driveways for 25-cents a load. Shortly after it was built, his brother Brian became involved in the garage.

Rob Oldfield, Brian's son, took over the garage in 1973 when his father was diagnosed with cancer. Though it interrupted his education (Rob had completed two years towards a Bachelor of Science degree at the University of Victoria), Rob has continued to run the garage and upheld its reputation for good service and community atmosphere. The business has continued to be successful, enough so that the garage – which was really an unheated barn with a leaky roof – was rebuilt and modernized. It still stands at the same place on West Saanich Road.

As well as running his service station, Rob Oldfield is a serious badminton player. He began playing at the Prospect Lake Community Hall when he was ten years old, and it has become such a passion that he now travels all over the continent to play in tournaments. He is a national umpire, a director on Badminton Canada's board, and vice-president of Badminton B.C. He followed in his uncle's footsteps, and designed an umpire's chair for the Commonwealth Games in 1994 that were strong enough to hold people climbing it, but light enough to easily be moved.

The garage has been in business for more than 60 years. At a time when so many chain stores have squeezed out the small, family-owned businesses, it has persevered. Both Barney's rotating house and his father's house are designated heritage buildings.

The rotating house on Old West Saanich Road (Courtesy Colin Barr)

A Spartan Life, A Rich Legacy

KRYLE C. SYMONS

(Courtesy St. Michaels University School, Archives)

Kryle Symons: 1908 – 1994

When the amalgamation between St. Michael's School and the University School occurred in 1971, it became the second-largest independent school in the province. At the time, St. Michael's had 170 students, and University had 130. While the University School was facing bankruptcy prior to amalgamation, after 1971 the school was able to expand their existing facilities, and continue to educate and employ people from all over the globe. With approximately 870 students currently enrolled from kindergarten through grade 12, St. Michaels University School has become an integral part of Saanich – and a good deal of the school's success can be attributed to the Symons family, who founded St. Michael's in 1910.

Kryle Symons Sr. was 24 when he immigrated to Canada with his wife, Edith. A graduate of Keble College, Oxford, he taught for three years in a one-room schoolhouse on Salt Spring Island. He earned $42 a month and lived in a primitive log cabin. Kryle Jr., the oldest of three sons, was born on Salt Spring in 1908.

Kryle Sr.'s first private pupil was Monty Bridgman. The Bridgmans asked the Symons to move to Victoria to continue tutoring their son; they did, and Kryle began to tutor other students. When he had six steady pupils and dedicated parents, he knew it was time to move to larger premises. In 1912, Francis Rattenbury, the prominent architect who designed the Parliament Buildings and the Empress Hotel, lent Symons the money for the construction of a house and a school on what is now Windsor Road, where the boys also had level fields on which to play.

By 1917, a third son, Michael, was born, and there were 12 students registered at the school. During the First World War, enrolment was so low that money was tight, and Kryle Sr. spent many summers doing roadwork or building fences to make money.

An article in the Oak Bay Star reported that Symons Sr. "believed in the Spartan life. He flung windows wide in winter and stripped needless blankets from the beds of boarders, and chided the boys when they shrank from opening the red-hot, old stoves in the classrooms. His own large, horny hands seemed impervious to heat."

The St. Michael's of old was a place of strict discipline. One student, who went on to become a federal cabinet minister, was beaten regularly every Friday for keeping a "disorderly locker." The school asked for perfectionism, and some people – including the Oak Bay Star – believed "that his half-century as a school teacher left an indelible imprint on the educational standards of British Columbia."

When Kryle Sr. died in 1965, Kryle Jr. was headmaster. Ultimately, he was a teacher for 27 years and a headmaster for 20. Both Kryle and his brother Ned had begun attending the school in 1918. After Kryle completed his education at Brentwood College, he joined the teaching staff at St. Michael's School.

Kryle Jr. married Joan Watts in 1936. About the same time that their first son arrived, Kryle's brother Michael joined the R.A.F, and was killed in action in 1942. Ned also joined the service, but Kryle Jr. was needed at the school: with his mother's increasing ill health, he and Joan took on increasing responsibilities at the school.

Throughout his life, Kryle was active in the community. He served for 16 years on the Oak Bay Recreation Committee, and for 60 years he was a member of the Arion Male Voice Choir. An avid boater, he spent many summers on his boat, "Waukesha."

Though the Symons lived in Oak Bay, their involvement with St. Michael's School was an invaluable contribution to the present St. Michaels University School. Without Kryle Symons, the junior half of the school would never have existed, and without his son's help in pulling it through the difficult years of the two world wars and a depression, the school would have disintegrated. The Symons' contributions to Saanich were a vital part of the community.

This biography has been sponsored by the

The Victoria Historical Society

Please visit our website at: www.victoriahistoricalsociety.bc.ca

In Search of Pheasants

THE OLDFIELD FAMILY

H.C. Oldfield, 1926 (Saanich Archives)

The Oldfield family

Standing in the entranceway of the Saanich Municipal Hall on Vernon Avenue is a section from a centuries-old Douglas Fir. Before the tree was made into firewood in 1929, it was 229 feet tall with a 35-foot circumference and was over 345 years old.

It belongs to the municipality because John Oldfield liked to shoot pheasants. If it hadn't been for the pheasants, John may never have come to Canada to live in Winnipeg, where he met his wife, Emma Inman. If he hadn't met Emma, then his son Clarence would not have been born. And if Clarence had not been born, he would not have been a Saanich council member at the time when the tree was cut down, and then he wouldn't have donated part of it to the hall.

When John was 22 his father sent him from his home in Norfolk to oversee the family's sugar plantations in Jamaica. The lack of pheasants and the hot climate didn't agree with John; he suffered from fevers and illnesses for a year before he heard about the excellent pheasant shooting in Canada. In 1879 he went to see the pheasants for himself.

John liked the country so much that he convinced several of his friends to also buy land in Manitoba. He became part of a successful real estate business called Oldfield, Kirby and Gardner, one of Winnipeg's most profitable finance and realty companies.

John bought 340-acres on the Saanich Peninsula in 1903, sight unseen. He sent his son Clarence to clear the land and supervise the construction of the family home. Clarence was the "hippie" in the family, and was happy to live in a shack while he cleared land, planted gardens and raised livestock.

Several changes took place between 1912 and 1914. John and Emma Oldfield retired and moved to Saanich to live in their new house, Norfolk Lodge. Clarence married Doris, a schoolteacher he had met in Winnipeg, and two years later they built a house across from Norfolk Lodge.

Clarence was a multi-tasker. As well as managing one of the most productive farms on the Peninsula, he served as a municipal councillor from 1924 to 1930. He founded the Fruit Growers' Association, an organization created because farmers were suffering from the low prices offered by the canneries. He also directed a jam and canning factory (supplied with produce from the Fruit Growers' Association) at 3940 Quadra Street, now designated a heritage building. Because the municipality refused to spend tax money on burial land, John rallied community members to invest in the property now known as Royal Oak Burial Park.

Clarence and Doris had four sons, but as none became a farmer, the Oldfields sold the land in 1948 and moved into the Oak Bay Beach Hotel. Today only six acres of the original 340 are connected to the Norfolk Lodge.

When Patrick Hoole purchased the property in 1948 he decided to remove the stump of the old tree, and it took 190 sticks of dynamite to dislodge it.

Strawberry pickers on the Oldfield Farm, 1946 (Saanich Archives 1984-11-7)

This biography has been sponsored by

The Royal visit of King George VI and Queen Elizabeth, 1939
(Saanich Archives 1998-4-1)

Commando training station on Feltham Road
(Saanich Archives 1981-5-13)

1936 - 1945

In May, 1939, King George VI and Queen Elizabeth visited Victoria just before the outbreak of World War II in September. Dozens of huts were built on the west side of Finnerty Road as housing and other facilities for the Canadian Officers Training Corps. The Normal School served as a military hospital from 1942 to 1946. 1939 also saw the construction of the Royal Oak Inn, designed by architect Hubert Savage. Water mains were installed along Tudor Avenue and Cordova Bay Road. By the end of World War II, Saanich's population had doubled to more than 20,000, and was about to boom again as servicemen who had trained in Saanich returned to make Vancouver Island their home.

Everything Except Chess
DOUG PEDEN

Doug Peden: 1916 - 2005

In the 1936 Berlin Olympics the Canadians and Americans were in a face-off for the gold medal in men's basketball. The American team was taller, but the Canadians were faster, and the shorter team planned to use speed to upset their opponents. But in 1936 the basketball courts at the Berlin Olympics were made of clay and dirt, and the rain had turned it into a muddy slop. Unable to dribble the ball, the Canadians lost whatever advantage they might have had. Still, they won the silver medal, the only Olympic medal Canada has ever won in men's basketball, and a large part of their success was due to Saanich resident Doug Peden.

Peden was the top scorer of the games and led the team to the final. In fact, his success in basketball and in almost every other sport he played, suggests that Doug Peden is the greatest athlete British Columbia has ever produced. He's been named to the Canadian, B.C. and basketball halls of fame, and the Victoria Sports Hall of Fame for cycling, rugby and basketball. He received an honorary Doctor of Laws degree in 1994 from the University of Victoria, and the Times Colonist rated him the greatest Vancouver Island athlete

of the 20th Century. He's been called an athletic wonder at basketball, baseball, cycling, cricket, tennis, swimming, rugby, and he once said that the only sport he didn't like was chess.

His career highlights include five national

The Peden brothers, Doug and Torchy, at Chicago Stadium, 1939
(Courtesy B.Duncan)

titles and a silver medal in basketball and seven international cycling titles. He won the junior city championship in track and swimming, was a member of Canada's junior tennis team, and played Triple A baseball.

After the Olympics, Doug and his brother Bill "Torchy" Peden turned their energy to international cycling in the now defunct six-day races, where a team of two cyclists took turns racing on an oval track for six straight days. When it was their turn to rest, the riders slept on mattresses in the infield, with a blindfold over their eyes to block out the stadium lights. Together, the brothers earned about $60,000 each winter on the racing circuit.

When Doug wasn't cycling or playing basketball for the Vancouver Hornets, he was playing baseball. In 1939 Peden was signed to the Pittsburgh Pirates, one of several barnstorming teams that toured all over the United States playing exhibition games.

When he stopped travelling, Doug married Trudy McVeeters, a clerk at a drugstore who he met when he hobbled into the store on crutches. He also began working for the Daily Colonist,

and soon began a 26-year-career as the sports editor at the Victoria Times.

His family was equally sports-minded. Torchy Peden competed in cycling in the 1928 Olympics, was inducted into the Victoria Sports Hall of Fame and presented with a solid-gold bicycle that is on display in the Toronto Sports Hall of Fame. His sister Margaret Peden was the first woman to jump four feet six inches in the high jump, and his sister Anna joined the RCAF and was one of six nurses trained to jump from planes for para-rescue. The family also owned Peden's Bicycle Shop and Peden Lane in Brentwood was named to commemorate the family.

Doug retired in 1981, a year after Torchy died of cancer.

Though Doug inspired hundreds of columns of newsprint, today's athletes have become millionaires and the fans have become forgetful; consequently, his success is often overshadowed by modern stars. But the Victoria Sports Hall of Fame at Saanich Commonwealth Place has created a certain piece of immortality for this versatile athlete whose achievements outnumber anything else seen today.

The Hard-working, Opinionated Critic

BILL KERSEY

William Charles Kersey: 1888 - 1986

Like many immigrants who came to Canada in the early 20th century, Bill Kersey arrived in Toronto broke and jobless. Other than one successful operation on an ill chicken that he'd performed as a child, he didn't have much farming experience; nonetheless, a stranger helped find him a job milking cows in Niagara Falls, and he supported himself with a variety of farm jobs over the next two years.

Then Kersey succumbed to the rumours about the riches to be made in the west. The rumours were largely just that, but he found or created plenty of occupations. He became a writer, a Saanich councillor, a farmer, a baker, and a deliverer. When he retired, he wrote articles for the Daily Colonist. He also wrote a memoir, *Ramblings of An Immigrant Boy*, that revealed the voice and sensibilities of an earlier generation.

When 18-year-old Kersey arrived in Victoria in 1906, the Empress Hotel was being built on stilts, Government Street was paved with wooden blocks, and women weren't allowed to enter

(Saanich Archives)

saloons. Oak Bay and Saanich had only recently been incorporated as municipalities. Electric streetcars were the main means of transportation and bicycles were left unchained.

Kersey soon convinced his girlfriend Nellie Brown to follow him to Victoria, and they married in 1910. Shortly after their honeymoon in England, Kersey began delivering meat for a butcher. He recalled that often the wagon would be piled so high that some sheep - the sheep were always placed on top - would fall off, and he would find them hanging on a fence on the return trip, placed there by a person passing by.

Kersey built a bakery in the area called Maywood, now the site of Mayfair shopping centre. It opened on April 15, 1912, the same day he heard that the Titanic had sunk. He hired a baker, bought a delivery van and a black mare. Soon he had to hire more staff, and a second delivery van. Through he and Nellie's hard work, they managed to keep the bakery going through the war.

In 1916, Kersey bought five acres on Stelly's Cross Road. He continued to work at the bakery until he paid off the property, but by 1919 he had sold the business, bought a cow, a sow, some chickens, and planted two acres of strawberries.

When strawberry prices suddenly took a steep dive, Kersey was looking for ways to increase his income, so he approached the circulation manager of the Daily Colonist with a proposal to organize carrier routes from Royal Oak to Deep Cove. The service began in 1924, and he woke up at four every morning, carried an axe and chain to clear the roads of fallen trees, hoped he wouldn't meet any stray cows, and completed every delivery over the next 37 years. He would finish at 8 a.m. and go to work on the farm, but it was the Colonist run that would keep the family off relief through the depression.

By 1942, Kersey became involved with the Saanich council, primarily to speed up Ward Six's secession from Saanich. In 1945 he was elected councillor, and by 1951, when Ward Six became Central Saanich, he retired from politics. Ever the critic of political procedures, he claimed his greatest achievement was acquiring cushions for the council's chairs.

In 1945, Kersey sold his farm in Saanich, and by 1961, he retired from the paper delivery business, and took up "loafing." Nellie was able to enjoy a few years of loafing before she died in 1958. Kersey remarried, and his second wife Mae, his two sons, three grandchildren, and eight great-grandchildren survived him when he died at 98.

Like many immigrants of the time, Kersey came to Canada to make his fortune, and was self-disciplined, hard working, and opinionated. He criticized the modern education and justice systems, the decline of physical punishment for children, the reluctance of people to volunteer, junk food, and "able-bodied youths on welfare." In one inflammatory statement, he wrote, "The sad state of society today can be laid squarely on the shoulders of psychiatrists and reformers."

However, despite his strong opinions, he readily acknowledged that his opinions were his and his alone. Much of Kersey's writing expressed a genuine regret for the loss of the community he'd known in earlier years, when strangers helped strangers, people who worked hard were rewarded, and fallen sheep were hung on fences, to ensure their safe retrieval.

Promoting Good Health, Good Books and Worthy Causes

W. & G. McGILL

Gertrude McGill: 1900 - 1980
William McGill: 1891 – 1994

Three months after William McGill's father died of a tetanus infection following a leg injury, an anti-toxin was developed that would have saved his life. That's when McGill knew he had found his calling, and decided to become a pharmacist. He became a co-founder of the McGill and Orme pharmacies, and though he sold his stock in the company in 1945, he continued to work in the Fort Street store until he was almost 100 years old.

Since the first McGill and Orme store was opened in 1930, the business has grown and there are now nine pharmacies operating under the McGill and Orme name on Vancouver Island. McGill's only time away from the profession was when he served as a flyer in the First World War. He retired in 1990, four years before he died at 103. Rather ironically, he attributed much of his good health and long life to never taking medicine.

William met Cyril Orme when McGill moved out west from Ontario. Orme wanted William to start a pharmacy business with him in Prince Rupert, but William wouldn't leave Victoria. Two years later, the two men came to a compromise: one McGill and Orme pharmacy was opened in Prince Rupert and another in Victoria.

Meanwhile, William's wife Gertrude was proving that sometimes the people with the greatest influence work in their own backyard. There, she built a miniature house with green trim, to-

gether with a jungle gym and sandboxes as tools for fostering knowledge, caring and a love of reading. Gertrude was concerned that children were trading books for comics, and wanted to encourage them to explore more literary material. To help make reading fun and interactive, she decided to build the "Book House" in the garden of her home on Tattersall Drive. The structure was large enough for an adult to stand up in, but had child-size chairs, tables and a chesterfield. The walls were lined with books donated by various Canadian publishers.

In the first year of the Book House's existence, 75 children attended to hear stories and play in the garden. The next year, 200 attended, and when the numbers continued to grow, volunteers stepped in to read aloud, and parents of children helped to build play equipment. By 1949, Gertrude and 50 parents from eight other Co-Op playgroups created the Vancouver Island Co-Op Play Group Association. The playgroup blossomed into today's Vancouver Island Co-operative Preschool Association, an organization in which an estimated 25,000 families have been involved.

Later, Gertrude became the preschool convener for the BC Teachers' Association, and served on the Victoria school board for 11 years, where she was involved in establishing a kindergarten program on Vancouver Island.

Gertrude was also involved in the Save the Children Fund (SCF): she served as the executive officer, honorary vice-president and Vancouver Island representative. Save the Children raised money for causes such as the meningitis epidemic in Austria, sponsorship of needy children and mother/child care centres in Thailand and Nepal and relief after earthquakes and other national disasters. It was her idea to ask children to collect donations as they went door-to-door on Halloween; in 1951, Victoria children became the first in the province to carry SCF cans.

Nellie McClung, a good friend of Gertrude's who nominated her for the position of school trustee, once described her as "a child-lover and a merry-hearted crusader, who is at the same time hard-headed as a bank manager and practical as a kitchen cabinet. She can, by her enthusiasm, light fires in cold places, and by her good sense, keep them burning."

(Courtesy McGill & Orme - Rexall)

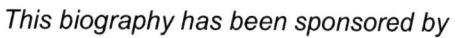 *This biography has been sponsored by*

The Sherman house on Seaview Road (Saanich Archives)

She Who Walks Quickly

DR. MARIAN SHERMAN

Dr. Marian Bostock Sherman: 1892 – 1975

Marian Sherman was a very fast walker. She walked so quickly that she almost ran everywhere she went, and her strong opinions, pork-pie hats and rapid stride made her a familiar character in Saanich.

It was fortunate that she moved quickly, because she had a lot of things to do. She was a doctor, a medical missionary, a wife, a mother and a humanist. She served as chairman of the Mental Hygiene for the Local Provincial and National Councils of Women, president of the

Anglican W.A. and the Greater Victoria Welfare Council, and president of the Victoria Senior Citizens' Welfare Association.

She was named Canadian Humanist of the Year shortly before she died in 1975. Other recipients of the award include Sue Rodriguez, the woman who went to the Supreme Court of Canada to fight for a doctor-assisted suicide, and Canadian author Margaret Atwood.

It's likely that Marian inherited many of her humanist characteristics from her father Hewitt Bostock, who was a Liberal. He was inspired by Cecil Rhodes in South Africa, who left nearly all of his fortune to public service, and tried to implement similar projects in B.C. But his finances didn't cover his progressive plans and eventually he had to resign his political seat and took up ranching in the Cariboo. In 1904 he became a senator, and in 1922 he became speaker of the senate. He died seven years later.

Marian was the eldest of eight children and was born in England shortly before the family immigrated to Canada. She grew up on Rockland Avenue in the house now known as "The Caroline Macklem Home." The Bostocks called it "Shuhuum," which means "windy place."

At 15, Marian was sent to school in England and became a medical student at St. George's Hospital in London. She was appointed house surgeon at St. George's during the First World War. She also became an interdenominational medical missionary, and in 1922 met her husband Victor in India. They married in 1928, lived in India until 1934 and settled at Ten Mile Point in 1936. They lived at Miramar on Seaview Road.

Marian became the leader of the Humanists in Victoria, and the next 40 years of her life were devoted to causes she felt strongly about, such as religion (she was a devout atheist) and abortion. She frequently uttered phrases like, "Belief is a prejudice instilled in youth. A believer is not a thinker and a thinker is not a believer."

Marian was highly controversial and wasn't shy about expressing her opinions. Her experiences in two world wars and working as a missionary in India gradually affected her opinion that a Christian God as suggested by the Bible could not be behind such events and conditions. Instead, she believed that people should look for – and would find – security and love among their fellow humans.

Marian had been the diocesan president of the Anglican W.A. and a member of St. Luke's Church, but she quickly discovered that when she tried to discuss her ideas with the clergy and other church members, "the wrath of heaven descended."

Many people disagreed with Marian's beliefs, but no one could disagree that she was a strong believer in the human spirit. And with a spirit like hers, it's perhaps not surprising that she had so much faith in the human race.

The Father of Modern Mapping

GERRY ANDREWS

Dr. Gerald Smedley Andrews MBE, B.Sc. Fr. 1903 –

When Gerry Andrews graduated from high school, a teacher said to him, "You might be interested in this new profession that has such a great future in Canada. It's forestry and it's going to be a primary industry."

The teacher was probably unaware that this information would lead Gerry to the beaches of Normandy, to the backwoods of B.C. and many places in between.

Gerry was born and raised in Winnipeg, but spent his childhood living in various parts of western Canada. In 1922, he earned his Teacher's Diploma, and spent four years teaching in the interior of B.C. until he had earned enough money to enroll in the Forestry program at the University of Toronto. In 1930, he graduated at the top of his class, with a bachelor's degree in forestry. Immediately after his final exams, he joined the B.C. Forest Service and became instrumental in developing aerial photography and applying it to forest surveying and mapping.

Pastel by Elizabeth R. Goward, 1980 (Courtesy G.S. Andrews)

In 1933, Gerry studied air surveying in Oxford, England and Dresden, Germany. He was trying to develop techniques to map the heavily forested areas of B.C., which, prior to aerial photography, presented an almost impossible task to surveyors.

In 1938, Gerry married Jean Bergthelmet, and Mary, the first of two daughters, was born a year later.

When the war broke out, 34-year-old Gerry was in northern B.C. doing vertical air photog-

raphy for the proposed Alaska Highway. Having experienced Nazism during his time in Germany, he immediately tried to sign up with the Royal Canadian Air Force, but they refused him. Undeterred, Gerald went to England where the British Army was happy to utilize his skills.

After he spent time serving with the Royal Engineers, the Canadians realized their mistake and he was transferred to the Royal Canadian Engineers, with the assignment to create special, small cameras using high-quality film for aerial surveying. He went from surveying land for a highway to being entrusted with ensuring safe landings for the D-Day invasion in Normandy. The Allies wanted maps of the contours of the ocean floor; they needed to know what depth of water the troops would wade through and where the landing craft would ground. The team worked day and night to create about 100 profiles, and Gerry was promoted to lieutenant colonel.

Meanwhile, Jean and nine-month-old Mary were alone in Canada, and had very little money. They were evicted from their home and Jean had to get a job as a file clerk. When Gerry came back from the war, Mary had already started grade one. Her sister Christine was born later.

In 1951, Gerry bought a house on Blenkinsop Road with 4.5 acres of orchards, rock gardens and exotic plants, where he also grew his own pipe tobacco. The family lived on Blenkinsop until 1980. During this period, he began to put together a book, entitled Light and Shadow, that was composed of 21 of his black and white sketches, and Highlights of a Long Life.

Gerry was B.C.'s longest-serving surveyor-general, occupying the post from 1951 until 1968, when he began a very active retirement. He served as a special lecturer for UVic, travelling all over the world to speak about aerial photography techniques. He was also a member and president of the B.C. Historical Society and wrote several dozen articles for the association. He wrote a memoir about his teaching experiences in the Cree-speaking community of Kelly Lake and wrote another book called Big Bar Country.

Gerry was made a Member of the British Empire and was named to the Order of Canada and the Order of British Columbia for his pre-eminence in surveying and mapping. He was also awarded an Honorary Doctorate in Engineering from UVic.

Gerry is now over 100 years old, and many people would agree that over the course of a century, he accomplished more than a lifetime's worth of achievements.

The Maltwood Legacy: OXO and Art
K. & J. MALTWOOD

(Courtesy Maltwood Art Museum & Gallery)

John Maltwood: 1867 - 1967

Katherine Sapsworth Maltwood: 1878 - 1961

While many people have placed a yellow box of OXO into their grocery cart, few know that a Saanich resident was involved in the invention of the bullion cube.

In 1938, John and Katherine Maltwood came to Victoria and bought the Royal Oak Inn from Florence and Colin Forrest. The Maltwood's re-named the building The Thatch after its thatched roof, and it became their home - and the showcase of Katherine's art collection - for over 20 years.

John Maltwood had passed the senior Oxford University entrance examinations when he was 14. He went on to make a fortune as a manager and inventor for the OXO Corporation. The OXO cube has an illustrious history. It was sent as emergency rations to soldiers in the trenches of World War I, Captain Scott carried OXO on his journey to the South Pole, and marathon runners in the 1908 Olympics drank it during the race. Today, the silver-wrapped cube is still a popular seller.

John's wife Katherine was a successful sculptor and exhibitor with the Royal Academy of London. In 1911 she released Magna Mater, her first sculpture to achieve notable success. She was a freethinking woman who disdained the prevailing idea that women should stay at home, and the sculpture portrayed a crouched, bound woman who had powerful arms and legs. It was considered a symbol for the women's movement.

Katherine was equally talented in her acquisition of art as in its creation; when John retired in the 1920's, the couple made several travels to the east. In addition to taking up Yoga and Buddhism, Katherine bought several Chinese paintings and ceramics, rounding out an art collection that some consider one of the best in Canada.

During World War I, Katherine did very little sculpting, possibly because she was too busy running a hospital for a training camp in Tadworth, England. She retired from sculpting in 1929 and devoted her time to studying archaeology and literature.

Her focus was Arthurian legends, and she spent nearly 25 years on a theory that certain roads, landmarks, footpaths and artificial waterways in Glastonbury formed giant figures of the zodiac - specifically, figures she believed corresponded with the leviathan creatures battled by King Arthur. While she was alive, experts in the field paid little attention to her work, but, as so often happens with artists, interest grew after she died in 1961.

Florence and Colin Forrest immigrated to Victoria from Shanghai in 1936. The Forrests commissioned Hubert Savage to build them a house built in the style of an English Tudor Inn, and it became the Royal Oak Inn at 4509 West Saanich Road. Unfortunately for the Forrests,

the Inn was short-lived. It opened in 1939, when gasoline rationing and other circumstances contrived to make the business unsustainable, and they were forced to close the business and sell the building in 1940 to the Maltwoods.

In 1964, John donated "The Thatch" and its accompanying art collection to the University of Victoria. The collection, now in the Maltwood Museum and Art Gallery at UVic, includes work by Emily Carr and Katherine (although many of her sculptures were destroyed during World War II when a bomb was dropped on the house in England that contained much of her work.)

In 1978, the collection was moved from the Thatch to the UVic campus, and the University sold the building and the accompanying six acres to Saanich Municipality. It is now leased to a restaurant.

The Thatch (Saanich Archives 1981-6-10)

The Tenacious Painter of People

MYFANWY PAVELIC

Myfanwy Pavelic: 1916 -

Myfanwy Pavelic is one of Canada's leading portrait artists, although she hates the term "portraitist" and prefers to be called "a painter who does people." Over the course of her career, she has painted many people, including high-profile subjects such as former Prime Minister Pierre Trudeau, actress Katherine Hepburn and violinist Yehudi Menuhin. She remains unapologetic for her representational style, even though she has been critisized for it and called an illustrator, not an artist. But then, Pavelic is unapologetic about most things.

When Pavelic won the commission to paint the official portrait of Pierre Trudeau to hang in the House of Commons, she refused to travel to Montreal and demanded that the Prime Minister come to her studio in Saanich instead. She risked losing the prestigious job, but she didn't back down. Some reporters said that it may have been the only time Trudeau ever bowed to the wishes of a westerner.

(Courtesy Times Colonist)

As the only child of Lillian and John Spencer, Pavelic's upbringing could explain her tenaciousness. Her grandfather was the owner of Spencer's retail stores (later sold to Eatons), and Pavelic enjoyed many opportunities and privileges that furthered her career. As a child, she made frequent trips to Europe, had private tutors and made her formal debut at the Royal Court where she was introduced to the King and Queen of England. After a disastrous marriage and subsequent divorce, her father paid for her to live in the famed Algonquin Hotel in New York, where she focused exclusively on her art. She never had to paint for a living.

But Pavelic had her share of challenges. She was born with a crippling joint disorder that kept her in a wheelchair as a child; her knee joints were shallow and didn't provide sufficient space for her knees to sit properly. As a teenager, she almost died when her leg became infected after knee surgery. Her joint disorder has continued to haunt her throughout her adult life.

She married lawyer Don Campbell when she was 23 years old. After their honeymoon, the couple returned to Saanich to live in the house her father had given them as a wedding present, but Pavelic hated the domestic life. Instead of sitting at home to contribute to the war effort by knitting for the soldiers, she took up her paintbrush and went on a tour across Canada, painting portraits and donating the proceeds to the Red Cross. Her husband thought it was a silly idea, but she raised $10,000. After she got back from the tour, she talked to her father who quietly arranged a divorce.

In 1948, she married Nikola Pavelic. Pavelic was the son of a high-ranking Yugoslavian cabinet minister who nearly lost his life when Tito rose to power in Yugoslavia. The communist dictator ordered that Nikola, as the son of an influential politician, be shot on sight. Stopped at the border, the guard checked his pockets and found a visiting card that actually belonged to one of Nikola's friends. The guard mistook Nikola for the man on the card and let him go.

Over the years, Myfanwy's joint problems have grown worse. She can no longer stand up to paint, and says if she can't stand, she can't paint. Despite trying several contraptions, including a drawing board with leather straps to support her, Myfanwy is unable to paint. The artist who was praised for capturing the spirit of her subjects and releasing it onto a canvas is once more fighting her joints to be able to do what she loves.

This biography has been sponsored by

(Courtesy Babe Warren)

Babe's Honey, Charlie's Bees
THE WARRENS

Alison (Babe) Warren: 1918 -
Charlie Warren: 1917 - 2003

Some of the images commonly associated with farms are rows of vegetables, ploughed fields and fertilizer. The less obvious but crucial part of the picture are the bees, because without them there would be no fruits or vegetables. In fact, the bee is so important that it was introduced to New Zealand and Australia to aid in the pollination of flowering plants. Bees are essential to the success of farms in Saanich, and for over 60 years, many of these insects have made their homes in the hives of Babe and Charlie Warren.

Honey has been called "liquid gold" and the "nectar of the Gods." It's mentioned in both the bible and the Qur'an. The ancient Egyptians used it to embalm their dead, treat mild burns and lacerations, improve fertility and stop hair loss. It was used as a food preserver in India and other Asian countries, and is widely used today as a sweetener in baked goods, fruits, cereals and medicines. And for over 60 years, thanks to the enterprise and hard work of two Saanich residents, the fluorescent labels of Babe's Honey have graced the pantry shelves of British Columbians.

Alison Smith (known as Babe because she was the youngest of five children) met Charlie Warren on a blind date in 1937, and they married two years later. Babe was a stenographer and Charlie was a sheet metal worker, but he had farming in his roots: his grandfather was pioneer farmer J.J. Pendray.

In 1943, Charlie was on a hunting trip with his neighbour, Charles West, who also happened to be a hobby beekeeper. The two found a nest of bees in a fallen log. The next day, the pair returned with chainsaws and buckets to harvest the honey. Their timing was excellent: sugar rationing due to the Second World War was in effect, and honey was a popular and lucrative alternative. In 1944, Babe's Honey was born – and it would become a lifetime occupation that Charlie described as a hobby, not a job.

The operation began as a four-hive, backyard business at their home on Lansdown Road, although their hives were moved to the Pendray Farm in Lakehill not long after. Eventually they would move the hives to their home on Walton Place, off Oldfield Road.

Babe's Honey has been a popular item on the shelves of Vancouver Island grocery stores for three generations. At its peak, the Warren's operated over 3,000 hives on Vancouer Island and the interior of B.C. and became the largest honey and beekeeping operation in the province. In 1992, they won the Farmer of Distinction Award from the South Vancouver Island Direct Farm Marketing Association. They also won the Canadian Honey Council Annual Award for Outstanding Contribution to the Industry.

While honey may be "liquid gold," beekeeping, like any type of farming, is subject to its trials. The weather is the primary danger (bees need a temperate climate) but bears and pests can also be a problem. The late 1990's were a particularly difficult time for the Warren's. They were forced to consolidate their business on Vancouver Island after a bee mite disease depleted their stock and forced a quarantine of the industry, and Charlie suffered a series of debilitating strokes before he passed away in 2003.

Despite the recent setbacks and the difficulties of working in a risky industry, the 87-year-old Babe is still running a successful business – and keeping as busy as the bees in their hives.

From Market Garden to the Wild Blue Yonder

JOE HOWROYD

Joe Howroyd

(Courtesy John Howroyd)

Throughout the late 1940's and early 1950's, Joe was a familiar sight in his yellow PT-26 Cornell ex-military trainer, gliding across Shelbourne Street to land among the fields of yellow daffodils on his family's farm.

Even during his early days as a student at the Model School (now the Young building of Camosun College), Joe was enthralled by the aircraft that operated from the Lansdowne airfield. He not only learned to fly, but eventually established the Daffodil Airstrip on his land. The airstrip ran from Shelbourne along what is now Mortimer Street to Gordon Head Road. The first flight in 1933 from this field was in a Pietenpol CF-AOG, which had been built by a friend, from the plans in a Mechanics Illustrated magazine. Later, he also flew a blue Stinson and a red and white Luscombe.

Joe's father, John Wilson Howroyd, immigrated to Victoria from Bradford, Yorkshire, England in the early 1900s. John Howroyd was an architect who practiced in Victoria until his physician insisted he take up farming as a cure for his emphysema. After a brief stint raising cows in Oak Bay, he established a market garden at the corner of Cedar Hill X Road and Richmond Road. John and his wife Mary (Booth) Howroyd had a daughter Grace, a son Joe, and a daughter Margaret. John also served as a Saanich councilor.

Joe recalled that one Christmas during the depression, their celery crop had failed and all they had to eat for dinner was Brussels sprouts. They were saved from this hum-drum fare by an unexpected knock on the door; the Lou-Poy family, who ran a vegetable wholesale business and often bought vegetables from the Howroyds to distribute to stores, had brought them a turkey.

Joe, a gifted but untrained mechanic, soon set about mechanizing the farm operation. The family purchased an additional parcel of 60 acres at the corner of Mortimer and Shelbourne Streets, running from Cedar Hill Road across Shelbourne to Gordon Head Road. The focus shifted to daffodil flower and bulb production, for which Joe created many ingenious devices, including a fork lift attachment for a Ford tractor, a bulb digger, a bulb grader, a sterilization tank and a hay bale loader. Thanks to these improvements, most of the work required by the farm could be done by Joe, his wife Iris (Button) and their young son, Johnny. Every year, Joe donated three truckloads of daffodil bulbs to the City of Victoria to be planted in Beacon Hill Park. They can be seen growing wild to this day.

Up until 1962, it was quite common to see aircraft lined up to take-off on land now the site of Campus View School. The airstrip was the hub of private flying until it was swallowed by development. It was common for Frank Copley and his family to fly from their airstrip (which is now the Northridge subdivision) to the Daffodil Airstrip for a cup of tea.

In 1953, Joe teamed up with Claude Butler and established another airfield off Keating Cross Road in Central Saanich. Despite constant excavation, the field is still used today, managed by Joe's son Johnny who exceeds even his father's passion for flight. Johnny now has five planes of his own and another airstrip, Raven Field, which is at Quamichan Lake near Duncan. Along with flying, his interests lay in constructing and rebuilding older airplanes. One of his most memorable flights was flying an old PPY 5A Catalina flying boat from Zimbabwe, Africa to New Zealand.

Howroyd Road in Saanich is a reminder of the impact this family had on Saanich over the years.

Joe Howroyd's Stinson CF-HUL at the Daffodil airstrip, Iris Howroyd on the far right
(Courtesy John Howroyd)

This biography has been sponsored by
The Saanich Sunrise Rotary Club
- meets for breakfast every Tuesday morning at 7:00 a.m.
at the de Dutch Pannekoek House at Quadra and McKenzie
Contact: Jan Brister at 381-2389

Grading at Saanich Road and McKenzie Avenue, 1948 (Saanich Archives 1983-8-2)

Saanich Health Centre, 1955 (Saanich Archives 1980-14-14)

1946 - 1955

Politics played a major role in Saanich in the late 1940s. After World War II, Saanich became a favoured settling area for soldiers granted land under the Veterans Land Act. To accommodate the new families in the municipality many residents supported a suggestion to amalgamate with Victoria. Though an amalgamation would mean an increase of municipal services for the growing population, those on the other side of the argument favoured the construction of a new municipal hall, fire and police complex, and were pleased with the creation of the Saanich Parks Department in 1948. While many supported amalgamation for the theorized financial benefits for Saanich, it would have meant compromising the balance of urban and rural living Saanich maintained. Reeve George Chatterton spoke for many residents when he said "My head says yes but my heart says no." In 1949, the ward system of representation was abolished, and the following year what had been Ward 6 was granted independent municipal status as Central Saanich. Residents elected Grace Shaw to council in 1951 and she served as the first female council member for two years.

From Dawn Till Dusk

RICHARD LAYRITZ

Richard Emil Layritz: 1867 – 1954

Richard Layritz was often described as a workaholic, a man who, even in his eighties, worked from dawn till dusk. Underneath the brusque German accent was a man who was liked and admired by his employees and was respected for his talent and his dedication – he wouldn't sell his plants to people if he didn't believe they would love and look after them. His wife Dorothy Giles once said, "The nursery is his hobby, his wife, his child, his everything." And it was his work ethic, his knowledge and his dedication that made Victoria the Garden City it is today.

Layritz was born near Dresden, Germany in 1867. He was the son of a textile merchant who had "agricultural leanings," and supported his son's love of plants by sending him to horticultural schools. After his schooling and apprenticeships, Layritz came to Canada because he heard the CPR travel propaganda about the glories of Canadian nature. He arrived in Montreal in 1887 at 19 and settled in Victoria a year later. He tried to start a small nursery near the Ross Bay Cemetery, but a particularly cold winter froze the plants, so he purchased 14 acres on Wilkinson Road. Clearing the land took almost a year, and Layritz ran out of money.

Richard then decided to join the Klondike gold rush as a packtrain man. He did this for a year, just long enough to pay off his debts. Not long after, the fruit tree business took off in the interior of British Columbia, becoming so profitable that Layritz opened additional nurseries in Kelowna, Vancouver and Gordon Head, and expanded the

Mr and Mrs Layritz, c1912 (Saanich Archives 1985-8-9a)

Wilkinson Road nursery to 75 acres. His nursery became one of the largest in the Pacific Northwest and he became president of the Pacific Northwest Nurserymen's Association.

Layritz travelled all over Europe to find new plants that would enrich the scenery of Victoria.

His work contributed to making Victoria the leading botanical centre in Canada. He shipped wild briar roses to Hong Kong, rhododendrons and azaleas to Japan, and many of his roses went to Portland, the "Rose City." His presence exists in the rows of flowering trees in downtown Victoria and the California Sequoia tree in front of the Parliament Buildings.

In 1906, Layritz returned to Germany and married Eliese Vetter, a 21-year-old who wasn't prepared for the rustic life in Victoria. When she died in 1916, some said it was of a broken heart. Richard married Dorothy Giles three years later, but they never had children. As Dorothy said, the plants were their children. Richard's influence on the landscape of Victoria and Saanich can still be seen in the numerous exotic plants, trees and shrubs in the area. He also provided the land for Layritz Park: Richard donated 10 acres, and later his widow Dorothy donated a further five acres of the Wilkinson Road property to Saanich for a children's park. Now, Layritz Park has a sports field, a clubhouse, and hosts a Little League team.

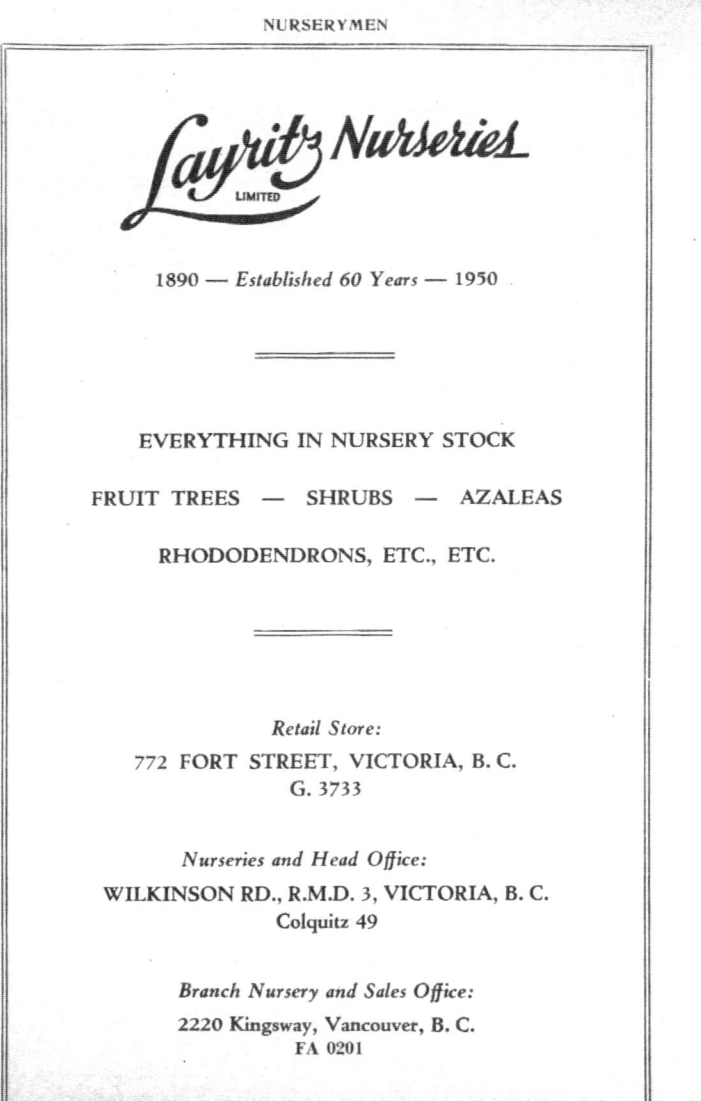

NURSERYMEN

Layritz Nurseries
LIMITED

1890 — *Established 60 Years* — 1950

EVERYTHING IN NURSERY STOCK

FRUIT TREES — SHRUBS — AZALEAS

RHODODENDRONS, ETC., ETC.

Retail Store:
772 FORT STREET, VICTORIA, B. C.
G. 3733

Nurseries and Head Office:
WILKINSON RD., R.M.D. 3, VICTORIA, B. C.
Colquitz 49

Branch Nursery and Sales Office:
2220 Kingsway, Vancouver, B. C.
FA 0201

843

(Saanich Archives)

A Sequoia tree, which Richard had planted from a seedling in 1889, has grown into a giant, living monument to the man who devoted his life to improving communities through the careful application of plants.

This biography has been sponsored by the  **Saanich** PARKS

Saanich Parks (250) 474-5522
www.saanich.ca

Canada's First Female Reporter

GWEN CASH

Gwen Cash: 1888 - 1983

When Gwen Cash arrived in Vancouver with a teacher's certificate, experience and glowing letters of recommendation, she expected to pick up where she had left off in England: teaching the ABC's to young children. When she was told she wouldn't be allowed to teach unless she went back to school for further training, she sat down with a pad of paper and a pencil and wrote articles about war-torn Britain.

She freelanced for various newspapers until she was hired by the Vancouver Daily Province and became the first female general reporter in Canada. She earned $90 a month, and continued to work as a freelance journalist for 65 years.

She met her husband, Bruce Cash, when she was in the Okanagan writing stories about the college students who volunteered their time as fruit pickers; with so many men fighting overseas, there was a shortage of farm labour. At the time, Bruce was an officer for the Rocky Mountain Rangers, although he worked at a variety of jobs, and was, at some point or another, a rancher, a turkey farmer, a machine mechanic and a game warden.

(Courtesy Times Colonist)

Gwen accompanied Bruce on many of his jobs, although her presence occasionally caused tension, particularly in the logging camps. Bruce was particularly piqued when Gwen smoked a cigar (to keep mosquitoes away) in front of several men. Another time she had to stay in town, away from the camp, because Bruce suspected her habit of wearing pants would cause an uproar. And when they lived on their remote ranch in Penticton, he warned her that her habit of sunbathing in the nude would land her in trouble someday. On the one occasion when a passerby stopped to ask for directions, Gwen calmly used a copy of the Saturday Evening Post for cover and gave the man his directions. Bruce and Gwen were married for thirty years, until Bruce died of a heart condition in 1947.

In 1937, Gwen became the public relations officer at the Empress Hotel and worked there for ten years. She left shortly after her second book, *A Million Miles from Ottawa*, was released. The CPR, who owned the Empress at the time, didn't approve of the book's unflattering reports of certain personages who patronized the Empress. After she left the hotel, her typewriter became her sole means of support.

Gwen is also well known in Saanich because of her home, which was known as Trend House, a unique polygonal building at 3516 Richmond Road. It was designed by architect John A. Di

Castri and sponsored by the British Columbia Coast Woods Trade Extension Bureau. Her house was built of hemlock and was the smallest of the ten at 830 square feet, but it received more discussion than any other: in the first year of its existence, more than 34,000 people came to see it.

Gwen wrote her memoir, *Off the Record*, when she was 86 years old (Myfanwy Pavelic painted the cover portrait.) She also began to write poetry and fiction. After her memoir was released, she said in an interview that the only thing she regretted about her increasing age was the lack of things to do. She said, "The worst thing about growing old is not being busy. I've done so much and worked so hard, I hate not being busy."

Gwen died in 1983 when she was 95 years old, ending a full and busy life as Canada's first female reporter.

This biography has been sponsored by

First Lady of Island Politics
NORA LINDSAY

(Courtesy Jamyang Lodto)

Nora Grace Lindsay: 1918 – 2000
Jack Lindsay: 1923 – 1973

As a young woman, Nora was independent and ambitious. She was born in Calgary in 1918, the oldest of four children. During the depression, she worked as a singing waitress at the famous Coconut Club. She was 20 when she spontaneously decided to visit Victoria, which she liked so much that she persuaded her family to settle there. Nora's family became good friends with their neighbours, the Lindsays. Their youngest son Jack wanted to marry Nora, but he

was several years younger than she was and she didn't take him seriously. She kept busy during the war and joined the Canadian Women's Army Corps, becoming one of the first women to get her wireless operator's licence. When Jack came back from the war, she had a change of heart, and they married in 1947.

Their first son was born in 1948, and at two years old was diagnosed with polio, an illness that would affect him throughout his life. Their second son was named Tim.

The 1950's was an infamous decade for women. When the Second World War ended and thousands of men came back to Canada, women were in the workforce in unprecedented numbers. Many married women faced intense criticism if they didn't give up their jobs for men, single women or widows. This, and the subsequent baby boom, created a period where female presence in the workforce slumped and the primary focus of home economic textbooks became teaching young women how to prepare for marriage.

Despite this environment, the 1950's were the years when Nora Lindsay earned several political achievements, reaching a pinnacle when she beat two male candidates to win the Progressive Conservative nomination for Saanich in 1953. She became the first woman to seek the Saanich representation in the provincial legislature on the PC ticket and was the first female candidate in Saanich politics. She also worked as campaign secretary to General George Randolph Pearkes and was campaign manager for George Chatterton in numerous federal elections.

Following a crippling strike, Nora was also an instigator in the formation of the current BC ferries structure. Before 1960, Vancouver Island was served mainly by the CPR ferries and the American-owned Black Ball Ferries that ran between Victoria, Port Angeles and Seattle. She created a petition and gathered information from sources like Hudson's Bay Company and Safeway Stores to convince the government that better ferry services were needed.

In 1963 she was elected to the Saanich School Board as a Trustee for five years, until her real estate business demanded more of her time. Her husband Jack (also known as 'Hap') was a Saanich Municipal employee. He worked in the building inspector's office and was the municipal assessor from 1957 until 1969. Jack died at age 50 in 1973. Nora initially retired to a house on the Gorge waterway and then to an apartment and finally a nursing home. She died at age 82.

This innovative woman's accomplishments were remarkable in that she raised a family while she made landmark strides into politics and business, at a time when women were still struggling to find their footing.

The First Mayor of Central Saanich

SYDNEY PICKLES

(Courtesy Municipality of Central Saanich)

Sydney Pickles 1894 – 1975

In 1950, change was afoot in Saanich. The residents of Ward six were becoming increasingly tired of labouring under a tax burden that financed city services they didn't use. The Ward system was in the process of being demolished. Sydney Pickles, a Saanich councillor and Ward six resident, refused to let the matter of secession go away, and to many people's astonishment, out of a 1951 plebiscite emerged a new municipality: Central Saanich.

Sydney Pickles liked to get his way. When he became Central Saanich's first mayor in 1951, he oversaw every detail of the administration of the new municipality. One year, he disapproved of some of the new fire chief's procedures, so he commandeered the municipal fire truck and hid it on a nearby farm.

Before Pickles served in the First World War as an aviator and test pilot, he had bought and farmed 400 acres on Mount Newton Cross Road. He raised crops and sheep until he sold the land in 1960 and donated part of the property to John Dean Park.

Pickles understood the frustration of his neighbours, who were paying heavy taxes for the police, schools and fire stations used primarily by more urban wards. Ward Six was approximately 12,000 acres of farms; sometimes it was referred to as the "forgotten" ward. Through the forties, dissatisfaction with the Saanich administration grew. A group of residents, including Pickles, met with the Saanich council on several occasions, but were refused a hearing. They tried to garner the support of the Provincial government, but the cabinet refused to get involved.

In 1948, an improvement tax reduced Ward six's taxes, but they still didn't receive any of the city services which the other wards did. Finally, a plebiscite to abolish the ward system was passed, and Reeve Warren of Saanich suggested that the plebiscite include the question, "Are you in favour of Ward Six seceding?" He expected that the answer would be no. To the astonishment of Warren and other Saanich councillors, the answer to the plebiscite was a resounding yes, and Ward Six suddenly became one of the largest municipalities in Greater Victoria.

Pickles was elected reeve (mayor) and held the position for four years. By many accounts, he was meticulous about overseeing every aspect of administration. Some people accused him of running a "one man" show.

After his term as mayor, Pickles left politics. In 1958, he organized the Handicapped Equipment Loan Association. As president, he helped hundreds of people suffering from arthritis and other disabilities remain mobile. He designed and built a variety of gadgets, and with the help of willing machine shops, created equipment for loan. There was no charge for the service, and people who used the equipment were under no obligations other than to return the equipment when they no longer needed it. In 1968, Pickles received the Good Citizen Award from the Native Sons of British Columbia.

Pickles designed and built his home Bryn-y-Mor on Newport Avenue in Oak Bay. He lived there for many years with his wife Adelaide Pickles, with whom he had two sons.

When Pickles died in 1975, the Times referred to him as "one of Victoria's most colourful personalities". The Sidney Review wrote, "Sydney Pickles will be remembered as the most dynamic figure in local politics the Peninsula has known. His every thought and action was to benefit the people he represented in the light of his firmest convictions. His work accomplished, he retired with dignity, never again seeking to influence those who followed".

This biography has been sponsored by
Saanich Archives - Geoff Castle, Municipal Archivist
780 Vernon Avenue, Victoria, BC   V8X 2W6   (250) 475-1775 ext. 3479
Open to the Public: Monday through Friday, 9:00 a.m. - 12:30 p.m.

A Voice for Veterans

LIONEL SPELLER

Lionel Speller

When Lionel Speller won a gold medal in wrestling at the B.C. Pro-Rec Championships in Vancouver, he competed in the featherweight division and weighed 125 pounds. When he came back from a Japanese POW camp in 1945, he weighed 97 pounds and had lost an inch in height.

Just as the seven Speller brothers' names were synonymous with sports, they became synonymous with military service: when the war broke out, one brother joined the RCAF, one joined the navy, two joined the army, and Lionel joined the Ordnance Corps.

Lionel's parents, Melville and Alexandra Speller, immigrated to Canada in 1910. In 1911, they settled on a piece of property on Carey Road. Lionel used to teach neighbourhood kids to box and gave them rides on his motorcycle. He originally joined the war as a shoemaker, but transferred to the Royal Canadian Corps of

(Courtesy Times Colonist)

Signals as a dispatch rider in order to be reunited with his bike.

In September of 1941, two Canadian battalions were sent to help the British defend their colony in Hong Kong, an exercise considered a "suicide mission". Most of the recruits hadn't finished training; Lionel had only three months of experience with an unloaded rifle and dummy hand grenades.

It was a disaster: of the 1,973 Canadians present, 290 died in battle, and another 260 died in hospitals and prison camps in Japan. Lionel Speller spent 44 months in captivity, much of it working in an open-pit iron mine in Suwa. Many prisoners suffered from diphtheria, malaria, and cholera. Their diet reduced them to skeletons: it consisted mainly of rice, and, as reported in an Islander interview, Lionel said that each day two men were allowed to gather grass and weeds to make soup for the 240 men in his section.

When the war ended and American soldiers liberated the Canadian troops, Lionel returned to Canada and settled in Saanich. In 1953, Lionel continued his involvement in the community and joined the "Spobbins" soccer team. The Spobbins were five Spellers and six members of the Robbins family who played a single match to raise money for Ken Griffin, a young man with polio.

Lionel married, had two children, and founded the B.C. branch of the Hong Kong Veterans Association of Canada. He remains a very active voice for the survivors of Japanese war camps who are seeking reparations. When Japan's emperor Hirohito visited the British Royals in 1998, Lionel organized letters of protest, as he had lobbied for years to get Japan to pay compensation to the POWs for their labour and suffering. He and other veterans also submitted compensation claims against Japanese companies who used prisoners as slave labour.

In 1952 the government paid the veterans compensation of $1 a day for each day they were in captivity. In 1998 the Canadian government paid the veterans an amount that totalled about $24,000 each, but Lionel publicly voiced the veterans' disappointment that the money came from Canadian taxpayers and not from Japan.

There were so many atrocities committed in World War II that it is difficult to remember, or do justice, to them all. But Lionel Speller has been a voice demanding that people not forget. He has fought for reparations for himself and hundreds of others across the country, and many people believe that makes him as worthy of his military medals as his work as a dispatcher more than 65 years ago.

A Saanich Icon

ADA BONE

Ada Bone: 1922 -

When Ada Bone was seven years old, she and her family were invited to a service at the German Lutheran Church. After the parishioners had finished singing the children's hymn "Jesus Loves Me," Ada stood up and raised her hand. Once she had the Reverend's attention, she said emphatically, "They're not singing the right words."

So the Reverend invited her to sing it the correct way, and she did - all three verses. When she was finished, her father told her to sit down, because the parishioners had not sung the song incorrectly - they had sung it in German. Though embarrassing, Ada's performance in church sparked the beginnings of a long and devoted music career, because after the service, the organist at the Church, Annie Denton, approached the Bone family and offered to give Ada music lessons. This would lead to a Diploma of Distinction Award from the Royal School of Music in London for her performance in the Royal Academy Music Examinations at the Empress Hotel when she was 15. Later, she became a member of the Christ Church Cathedral

(Courtesy Saanich News)

choir, and frequently performed solos.

Ada Bone is a life-long Saanich resident. Her parents, William and Virginia Burt, settled in the Prospect Lake area, where Ada was raised. At the time, there were only two other children besides

Ada in the area. Once a month, two constables (Elwell and Cummings) from the Saanich Police department made their rounds, and always carried candy to give to the three children.

Ada grew up in a slightly more exotic Saanich than the one that exists today. On Quadra Street there was a fox farm. On Saanich Road there was a zoo, complete with lions and tigers. There was also Featherland, an avian sanctuary run by Cecil and Adele Hyndman. Cecil was known as the "Bird Man," as his singular mission in life was to teach birds to talk, and he was often successful - Ada recalls "Itchy" the talking crow appearing on the CBC numerous times.

During the war years, Ada arranged concert parties to entertain the various camps of soldiers on southern Vancouver Island. She also entertained on a barge in the inner harbour. While it was a fun and exciting time, she always had to wonder how many of the men would come home.

Ada married Jim Bone in 1955 and moved to Donald Street in the Gorge Road area of Saanich, where she still resides today. Tragically, her husband died of cancer when their son Jim was only eight months old, and their son Stephen five years old. Though she was a single parent for most of her children's lives, Ada continued to volunteer and work on various community projects.

Ada feels her greatest accomplishment is the crosswalk at the corner of Tillicum and Obed Roads. She felt there were far too many collisions occurring at the corner, and worked for four years, collecting signatures and lobbying the municipality, to get the crosswalk. She is also proud of the several months she spent researching the history of "Hampton Hall," and the successful case she presented to the Saanich Council that the 1923 structure should be a designated heritage building.

For 10 years, Ada served on the Saanich Special Events Committee. She volunteered at the Strawberry Festival and various other fundraisers, and at the festival in 1993, former Mayor Murray Coell presented her with a set of Saanich bookends as a token of appreciation for her hard work and dedication.

Throughout her 83 years in the community, Ada Bone has retained the spirit of the little girl who raised her hand in a roomful of people to say, "Excuse me". And it has been to the benefit of Saanich that people have listened.

This biography has been sponsored by
The Horticulture Centre

A Passion for the Ordinary

URSULA JUPP

Ursula Jupp: 1903 – 1988

The stories of local farmers, seamen and road names fascinated Ursula Jupp. She wrote dozens of articles, four books, and devoted hours to interviewing and researching subjects usually bypassed by historians. She was a devoted history buff who transmitted her passion to the page, where readers could experience her enthusiasm and see that the stories of ordinary people were as important as those of any world leader.

As the daughter of a Saanich pioneer, Jupp had an intimate knowledge of Gordon Head that made the experiences of the early farmers immediate; from the menace posed by predators to livestock, to the arduous days of farming before irrigation, she provided a first-hand account of pioneer life.

The foreword to her fourth book states: "Ursula Jupp has laboriously chronicled the lives of a handful of men and women with a curious claim to fame. By all the rules of most history books they were nonentities: they commanded no armies, sent no men to their deaths, ruled no empires and with few exceptions took little part in history-making decisions. Yet what they did was more decisive for history than the many acts of statesmen who basked in higher glory."

(Saanich Archives)

Jupp's books, all self published, never became best sellers or won awards. One of her closest encounters to celebrity came when she was the first female editor of Victoria High School's newspaper, and Bruce Hutchison, Canada's longest serving journalist, was her assistant.

She served for a number of years on the

Saanich Heritage Advisory and Archival Committee, and was instrumental in forming The Friends of the Dodd House Society. She was one of the first female members of the Thermopylae Club and the Victoria Maritime Museum. But it wasn't these things that made Jupp particularly distinctive.

Jupp's extraordinary skill was seeing the interesting in the ordinary, and in her ability to be truly captivated by these things. In fact, her very first published story was about the widening of Shelbourne Road. She was taking a journalism class, heard about the road and created a two-part article about an otherwise humdrum event.

Jupp was born on the Scilly Islands. Her father, William Edwards, had to leave his daffodil farm because the income it generated couldn't sustain his family and the family of his older brother. So Edwards, his wife, Ursula and her sister settled in Gordon Head in 1912 on 16 leased acres. Edwards grew strawberries and became the first commercial daffodil grower in Gordon Head.

Jupp obtained the highest grades in B.C. when she passed her senior matriculation, and went on to attend the Normal School (now Camosun College). She graduated with a teaching certificate.

Jupp married William Edwards-Lay in 1923 and they had two daughters. Several years after their marriage ended, Ursula met Frank Jupp, chief engineer of the cableship Restorer. He died in 1950, but his occupation had sparked her interest in her sea-faring heritage and she wrote two books about deep-sea stories from the personal accounts of Saanich residents.

In 1975 she published *From Cordwood to Campus in Gordon Head, 1852 to 1959*. Her last book, *Cadboro Bay, A Ship, A Bay, A Sea-Monster*, was completed only a week before she died.

Jupp didn't rock the world, but her writing reminded readers that the history of their community was as interesting as the gold rush in the interior or the politics in the East. Her work has proved invaluable to writers, historians and citizens who want to learn more about Saanich.

The Maverick Photographer

JIM RYAN

(City of Victoria Archives PR73-6024)

Jim Ryan: 1920 – 1998

A news photographer must frequently take pictures of celebrities, royalty, politicians and other personalities. And sometimes, the photographer's personality overshadows the subject's, as frequently happened when Jim Ryan, or "Big Jim," was behind the camera. At six foot two and 280 pounds, Ryan was a big man, with a bigger personality. With his pork-pie hat, ever-present cigar and cumbersome Speedgraphic camera, Ryan became something of a legend during his 40 years as a photojournalist in Victoria and a resident of Ralph Street in Saanich.

For many years of his life, Ryan was an aggressive alcoholic. He was a brilliant photographer, but he could be difficult to work with. His determination to get the photo at any cost and his strong opinions alienated some people, yet he had many witnesses to his kindness and good humour.

Ryan was born in 1920 in Regina, Saskatchewan. He was the sixth child, and ultimately, there would be 13 people living in the family's four-bedroom house. Growing up in the depression meant all the Ryan children began working at a young age to bring money into the household. Ryan's first job was selling newspapers on street corners. When he was 14 and had only an eighth-grade education, he quit school and got a $5-a-week delivery job with the Chicago Photo Supply. Over the next six years, he was promoted and began to develop and print film. By the time World War II began, he was proficient in the darkroom.

At the beginning of the war, Ryan joined the navy and was posted to Esquimalt. He returned home in 1942 to marry his childhood sweetheart,

Patsy Webster. After the war ended, the navy began a photo section, and Ryan quickly signed up. He took photos of damaged ships that arrived in Esquimalt, special functions, visiting celebrities and other publicity events.

Before Ryan had joined the navy, he'd never had a drink or a cigarette, but before long he became an alcoholic with an addiction to cigars. He was also reputedly a "ferocious" fighter, and the more he drank, the more he fought. He spent several nights in jail for fighting.

The navy wasn't quite sure what to do with him; while one officer wanted him discharged, another recommended that he be promoted to Chief Petty Officer. Ryan had also been doing some freelancing for the Victoria Daily Colonist, so when the city editor wrote a letter to the navy promising full-time work, they let him go with an honourable discharge.

When Ryan started at the Colonist in 1949, he was almost 30 and had four children. He was paid $55 a week. He proved to be extremely dedicated, and worked far beyond the eight-hour day required. He was often the first at the scene, at any time of day or night, partly because he had an illegal police radio, but also because he had numerous informants who would phone him the moment a newsworthy event occurred.

But the newsroom seemed to be as conducive to drinking as the navy. Ryan was sometimes referred to as "the White Mayor of Chinatown" because of how much time he spent drinking,

gambling and eating in the Fisgard Street area with other Colonist staff. Despite his tremendous work ethic, the complaints from some citizens and reporters became so frequent that the Colonist fired him in 1953.

That same year, Ryan quit drinking and returned to freelancing. His work appeared in the Colonist, the Vancouver Sun and Province, Liberty Magazine, the Toronto Star Weekly, Maclean's, Time, Life and Beautiful B.C. magazines. In addition to freelancing, he became the official photographer for former Premier W.A.C. Bennett.

Ryan and his second wife, Hazel Martin, moved to Saanich (on Ralph Street) in 1961, where they lived for many years. Ryan extended his photographic skills into another venue, and was involved with the publication of several books, including *The Maverick Nun*, about a nun who cared for abandoned animals. He compiled a tribute – *My Friend* – in Premier Bennett's honour. He also did the photography for the book "Around Victoria and Vancouver Island."

When Ryan died in 1998, he had more than a quarter-million photographs in his collection. Reg Reynolds, a reporter at the Colonist, had written Ryan's biography. And even though it's been years since Ryan succumbed to cancer, he is still considered one of the best photographers the city has ever had.

This biography has been sponsored by **Black Press**

It Started with One Backhoe

JOHN CHEW

(Courtesy John Chew)

John Chew

Chew Excavating, which celebrated its 50th anniversary on January 19th, 2005, began on the advice of a friend. John Chew had worked for a while digging drainage ditches, so when a friend said that a backhoe could make the job easier and he could earn $8 an hour income at the same time, he paid attention. He managed to buy one, and obtained his first job: digging the sewers for Esquimalt, as the municipality didn't have its own backhoe at the time.

Since John's first backhoe, he has branched out into many other business interests, including ARC Asphalt Recycling, the huge road recycling train often seen working on highways, to Victoria's harbour ferries, which transports thousands of passengers and is a popular tourist attraction. He was also one of the founders of the Island Equipment Owners' Association. With only 12 members in 1964, the association has grown to include more than 150 members. However, John is still chairman of the Chew Excavating board, and the business is still his main focus and biggest enterprise. The company now specializes in installing major sewer lines, many of which service municipalities on Vancouver Island.

John was one of 11 children, and having three brothers and eight sisters. His father was pioneer farmer Chew Dang. All of the children helped out at their father's farms on the corner of Oldfield and Brookleigh Roads and in the 4800 block of West Saanich Road, which John eventually turned into his company's equipment yard. As a young boy, John recalls walking to the old Prospect Lake and Royal Oak Schools, unless he got a ride with Frank or Norm Copley in their two-ton wood truck.

The family struggled through periods when farm income was unpredictable. At one point, the Chews were unable to pay the rent for their property at 4846 West Saanich Road, and were forced to move into the barn across the street. John remembers that there was an old tin chimney that sat in the middle of the barn, and still wonders how it managed not to burn the building down.

John often found it difficult, as many did, to find work. There were some people who would offer work to minorities, and others who simply wouldn't. He says that Frank Copley was one of his first customers to give him a break, and the Chew and Copley families are still friends.

One of John's first jobs was with the Saanich municipality. There, John met Maurie Foster who was the dispatcher/time keeper for the Saanich Municipal Yard at the time. Maurie and his wife Eleanor had six daughters and one son, David Foster, the well-known producer. Maurie mentioned to John one day that his daughter was graduating from Sprott Shaw College and needed some work experience. John agreed and she not only earned work experience but eventually became Senior Vice-President. She was one of his many long-term employees; her career with Chew Excavating lasting more than 38 years. In fact, many people said that while John made the big decisions, it was Maureen that employees and customers had to keep happy.

Over the last 50 years, Chew Excavating has worked on many projects in Saanich and the Greater Victoria area. John Chew's company has been responsible for excavation work at the Town and Country Shopping Centre, the B.C. Tel (now Telus) building at Quadra and McKenzie and much of the sewer work in the Gorge area. He also worked on the Mayfair Mall and Hillside Mall. He installed the Sidney sewer system and built the Memorial Parkway in Langford. He is currently working on the Sooke sewer system. He has also installed many of the main gas lines, including the one from Sidney to Langford and UVic.

Over the years, John has supported many local sports, including the Saanich Hornet football team from 1968 to 1978. At about this time, John became overextended and nearly lost his business. Most of his equipment was auctioned off, and he had to start from scratch. Though it was difficult, he successfully rebuilt his company, which is now more successful than ever. Not bad for a member of a visible minority who started off with one backhoe.

This biography has been sponsored by

575 Gorge Road East, Victoria, BC V8T 2W5
Phone: (250) 386-7586 Fax: (250) 386-4550

Public Works Employees, 1957 (Saanich 1980-15-248)

An outing to the Butchart Gardens (Saanich Archives 1980-14-13)

1956 - 1965

Significant park development in the 1950s and 1960s led to increased recreational services in Saanich. Layritz ball park opened in 1958 on donated land, and the next year property for Gyro park was purchased. Nine acres of land owned by the Mattick family was rezoned for a pitch-and-putt golf course and the municipality laid plans to develop the Lambrick farm into a future park. The Urban Containment Boundary was established to manage growth in the municipality, and has played a significant role in shaping Saanich for past and future generations. In 1961 the new Police and Fire station was built on Vernon Avenue, where the new Municipal Hall would be located four years later. The transition of classes from the Lansdowne Campus to the Gordon Head Army Camp property was underway by 1961 as the University actively purchased land to accommodate its growing student population. B.C. Ferries commenced service between Swartz Bay and Tsawwassen in 1960, leading to a dramatic increase of visitors to the region. With tourism booming and the university growing annually, it came as no surprise when Saanich matched Victoria in population in 1965, then surpassed the capital city one year later

(Courtesy Lissa Calvert)

Restoring the Wetlands
GIFF CALVERT

Giff Calvert: 1912 – 1997

Innumerable animals and insects live in areas classified as "wetlands," land that includes swamps, bogs, ponds and marshes. In addition to providing habitats to these creatures, wetlands play an important role in maintaining the world's water supply. They also filter pollutants, prevent soil erosion and remove and store greenhouse gases from the atmosphere. According to Environment Canada, the country is home to 24 per cent of the world's wetlands, but development, farming, pollution and aggressive non-native plant species are causing these habitats to disappear at an alarming rate.

In the Prospect Lake area, a 20-acre parcel of land named Trevlac Pond Municipal Park serves as a reminder that careful environmental stewardship can preserve – and restore – wetlands and other threatened habitats. Long before the Canadian government implemented the national wetland conservation policy in 1991, Gilbert (Giff) William Calvert was working under his own initiative and using his own funds to return his property to its natural state. The result – Trevlac Pond – is a rich habitat for plants, birds, fish and other species that had long ago been driven out by drained land and grazing cattle.

Giff's lifelong passion for birds and their habitats began when he was a child growing up in the Yorkshire countryside in England. He completed his studies at Oxford University and married Sheila Mary Cunningham in 1938. They had three daughters, all of whom were born in England. The family immigrated to Canada in 1948 and moved to Saanich in 1968, when the four-year search for suitable property began. Giff eventually found the perfect spot on Prospect Lake Road. The property had been farmed, and was still being grazed by horses. However, Giff saw potential: the meadow still flooded every winter. The Calverts purchased the property and the accompanying 100-year-old house.

Giff then had a dam built to flood the meadow, and named it Trevlac Pond ("Calvert" spelled backwards.) He had deep channels built to accommodate diving birds and otters, while Trevlac Creek was trenched and terraced to provide spawning grounds for trout. In the end, the pond attracted far more than waterfowl. Otter, mink, muskrat and (for a short period of time) even a beaver made Trevlac Pond their home. More than 30 years later, the vegetation that once grew around the pond has returned, and the number of resident and migratory birds seen at the pond has increased from 79 species in 1972 to 160 species in 2000.

While Giff was building a nature sanctuary, he was still involved in his real estate career. After 30 years in the business, he retired in 1986. He and his dog Trev took daily walks on the trails and conducted impromptu tours for visitors. He sold the property to Saanich for $268,000, and on June 1, 1988, it became Trevlac Pond Municipal Park and a nature sanctuary. He said he sold the land because he wanted other generations to be able to enjoy it, and pointed out that as the property is only a short distance from town, it offers a tranquil and peaceful wilderness to a large, city-dwelling community.

During his lifetime, Giff served as a director, chairman or vice-president of many environmental societies and committees, and was a member of the Saanich Parks Committee from 1983 to 1997. While a member of the parks committee, he promoted the acquisition of wetlands and rational land use that would preserve the maximum amount of wildlife habitat. In 1995, he received the B.C. Individual Environmental Award for his contributions to preservation and for his efforts to educate people about their role in environmental stewardship; that the wetlands are not only important to the species that live in them, but also play a major role in the carbon cycle and global climate, and therefore to the maintenance of a sustainable ecosystem.

Pennies for Peggy
PEGGY WALTON PACKARD

Peggy Walton Packard: 1914 –

Peggy Walton Packard has been called Victoria's beloved doyenne of figurative sculpture, but she employs her creative powers on far more than sculpture. For decades, she has enthralled the community with her talent for music, theatre, gardening, teaching, and, of course, sculpting.

Many of her works are figurative sculptures of children, either as individuals or sculptures that interact with one another. In her garden, you might come across Hansel and Gretel or Narcissus. She has frequently been praised for her ability to capture emotion.

Over the years, Peggy has gathered a devoted following of students and art lovers. She taught art to many people in the Greater Victoria area, principally at high schools, community centres and at The Barn on Lansdowne Road. One artist and former student said in a Times Colonist article that "She would come to school, always a bit late, on her big

(Courtesy Times Colonist)

old men's bicycle wearing a sort of a cloak with two or three dogs behind her."

Peggy was born and raised on her father's four acre farm on the Lansdowne slope in Saanich. While the property is now much smaller, she still lives and teaches there today.

Her art career began in the 1930's when she enrolled in an art class and was immediately entranced by a bowl of clay. For five years, she lived in Philadelphia to attend the Pennsylvania Academy of Fine Arts, and also attended the famed Juilliard School of Music in New York. Since she returned to Victoria, her world-class talents have been devoted to the local art scene.

She is probably best known for the concrete sculpture of Queen Elizabeth II that was once displayed in Beacon Hill Park. In 1959, Peggy charged a modest $350 to create the 750-pound bust of the Queen. It was a sculpture intended to commemorate the royal visit in June of that year, but problems arose when Esquimalt and Oak Bay didn't want to pay their share of the statue's cost. The price, when landscaping was included, had escalated to $1,000, and two of the area's four municipalities had backed out of their share of the costs.

The city delayed paying Peggy her commission, and so the Victoria Daily Times launched a "Pennies for Peggy" campaign. The newspaper published headlines asking for people to donate pennies, which would be pushed to City Hall in a wheelbarrow. It proved the incentive the city needed, who announced the date that Peggy could pick up her cheque. However, the statue's misadventures weren't over yet. The day before Peggy was to pick up her cheque, the statue was stolen from City Hall and nine pennies were left in its place. Though the statue had taken many hours of Peggy's time, she was amused by the irony – now the city would have the landscaping, and no statue. City officials were less amused: one declared the kidnapping a "tragedy" and an insult to the Queen.

Fortunately, the statue was recovered three days later. One shoulder had suffered a shallow groove, but otherwise, was unharmed. It was then moved to a private office. On March 21, 1960, the statue was moved again to the south edge of Beacon Hill Park's main parking lot on Circle Drive, sans ceremony or public announcement. It was an ignoble beginning of an ignoble end for the statue, which received various indignations over the following months, culminating with the disappearance of the head, later found at the bottom of the Inner Harbour.

But the Daily Times stepped in, and commissioned a replacement made of bronze from Ottawa sculptor Arnold Price (the only Canadian sculptor with experience in bronze.) He used Peggy's original mould, and in 1962, the statue was installed near Queen's Lake on Circle Drive, a far prettier location than the parking lot, and in a material that has stood up well to vandalism.

As an artist and a teacher, Peggy Walton Packard has long enriched our local culture.

Flowers Scent by Air

BILL MATTICK

Bill Mattick: d. May 9, 1985

Bill Mattick was a character, and he knew it. So when Florence Pratt wrote a feature on him for the Daily Colonist in 1977, he told her to "tell it as it is, warts and all." And she did. She described his office, complete with pictures of racehorses on the wall hanging next to Playboy calendars, and among all the glowing material that discussed his successful farm and flower business, she also wrote, "He is a connoisseur of breasts." When she asked him what it was that made him appreciate them so much, he said, "Why not?"

"Why not" could have been Bill's motto. Why not open a roadside stand to sell passersby his extra farm produce? And when that stand took on a life of its own and grew into a popular tourist attraction with sunken gardens, a golf course and petting zoo - why not add a miniature steam train and pony rides?

He started farming in the Gordon Head area when he was 19 years old, on the 300 acres that now hold the University of Victoria. He sold that parcel of land to the government and bought 83 acres in the Cordova Bay area, which promised more water and less wind than the Gordon Head property.

In 1948, Bill became the first farmer to use air freight to ship flowers. In a landmark shipment, he sent more than 72,000 daffodils from British Columbia to Toronto. He traveled as far as Halifax on sales trips, and in the process

promoted tourism; he coined the popular slogan "flowers scent by air". In addition to operating his business, he served as a volunteer weather observer for 18 years.

But it wasn't until 1958 – when Mattick opened a roadside vegetable and fruit market to sell extra produce – that the farm began to expand. Within three years of building the roadside stand, the farm became the home of a menagerie of animals, including monkeys, goats and donkeys, and a miniature steam train that children could actually ride on followed shortly after. In 1962, he built a par-3 golf course and driving range. Bill had lost his hand and most of his arm in a farm accident when he was four years old, but it didn't stop him from enjoying golf, and apparently "the old man with a hook could hit a long ball".

Though Mattick sold 50 acres of the farm in 1969 to San Juan Development (although some people claim he lost it in a poker game) he continued operating the golf course and other attractions for another three years, until 1972 when his health began to decline. He was diagnosed with cancer, and underwent three surgeries within 15 months. His wife Joey, with whom he had two daughters, had died in an accident several years earlier.

Thanks to Bill and his "why not" attitude, his farm at 5271 Cordova Bay Road has become a staple in the Saanich Community. Today, the golf course is named Cordova Bay, and its club restaurant is named after Bill. Inside the restaurant is an interactive, life-size figure that resembles

(Courtesy Times Colonist)

Bill, complete with a cigarette between its lips and a bottle of Black Russian, his favourite drink, beside him. The figure has robotic elements, and occasionally the knee twitches or the feet sway, mystifying the restaurant diners who can never be quite sure if it moved or not. It's exactly the type of quirky, mischievous addition to the farm that Bill probably would have smiled at, shrugged, and said, "Why not?"

This biography has been sponsored by the
Cordova Bay Community Association
Roger Stonebanks – President   (250) 658-5125

A Fundraiser with Charm

ERIC CHARMAN

Eric Charman: 1932 –

Eric Charman has a talent for persuading people who can spare it to give money to worthy causes that need it. As an auctioneer, philanthropist, volunteer and master of ceremonies, Eric Charman has helped raise millions of dollars for charity and the arts. He has conducted more than 200 fundraising auctions in the Victoria area, and has been a principal fundraiser for the Victoria Symphony Foundation and the Pacific Opera; he has also been involved with various humanitarian causes, including World Refugee Year, the Community Chest and United Appeal.

Since he came to Canada more than 50 years ago, Eric has garnered the reputation of a *bon vivant* who isn't afraid to shake down the traditions of Victoria's establishment. As an outsider, he had to fight his way into the cliquey network of the Victoria Real Estate Board. He not only became known as the "realtor for the rich," but he and his 36-acre estate near Elk Lake have played host to people like Wayne Gretsky, Prince Edward and Gene Hackman.

(Courtesy Times Colonist)

Though Eric has become very successful, he wasn't born into the upper echelons of Victoria society. He was born in England in 1932, when the stereotypes and pressures of the time lead his mother to place him in an orphanage, and he was raised in foster homes. When he arrived in Canada in 1952, the 21 year old had some savings, but few job prospects. He worked for three months for his sponsor, a chicken farmer in Duncan, before moving to Victoria.

In archetypal rags-to-riches fashion, Eric charmed his way into a job at a trust company, a business that he knew nothing about. By 1959, he became a real estate agent with Fairfield Realty (renamed Charman Pacific in 1965.) He confounded the old boys' network who tried to deny him membership to the Victoria Real Estate Board by hiring a lawyer, and eventually became the only person to have served as president of the board on three occasions (1972, 1974 and 1976.) His also served terms as president of both the BC and the Canadian Real Estate Associations.

Eric married Shirley Wallace, and they currently live on a 36-acre estate with a 4,700-square-foot home called Donnington Farms. They have one son, Wallace, and grandchildren.

While Eric has raised millions for good works, it hasn't made him immune against occasionally offending people. In one notable instance in 1985, he arranged for 150 guests to attend a fundraiser for the Mustard Seed Food Bank at his estate. He had purchased latex gloves for his guests, who wore them in order to throw fresh cow dung at his silver Rolls Royce. People who weren't involved in throwing dung could watch from a helicopter that hovered above. While the event raised $3,800, some people felt it was tasteless and offensive (the Victoria Rolls Royce club was particularly perturbed.)

But by and large, Eric has received wide approbation for his work, and has numerous provincial and national awards to show for his efforts. In 1993, he was granted the Edmund C. Bovey Award for outstanding contributions to the arts. In 1995, he was named an Honorary Citizen of the City of Victoria, and in 1998 he was granted an honorary Doctorate of Laws from the University of Victoria. He was also named to the Order of British Columbia in 1999 and to the Order of Canada in 2000.

Whether he is serving as chair of the Victoria Symphony Foundation or raising money for the SPCA, Eric Charman employs the same tenacity he used when building a successful career from scratch. As Victoria's premier fundraiser, he serves as an example of what can be accomplished when people decide to support a worthy cause.

This biography has been sponsored by

W.D. Michell's potato crop (Saanich Archives 1981-19-91)

The Backbone of the Saanich Peninsula
THE MICHELL FAMILY

Thomas Michell: 1832 – 1916
Margaret Jenkins: d. 1912

Margaret Michell always rode sidesaddle, whether she was travelling to Victoria to sell her prize-winning butter, or going to a neighbour's house to employ her rudimentary midwifery or nursing skills. Although there is no record that Margaret ever received any medical training, she served as the area's local nurse and midwife and was apparently much beloved by her neighbours, who called her the "Lady of the Valley." She was always available to help a sick neighbour, even though she bore sixteen children (only six of whom survived), performed daily farm chores and sold the extra produce.

Her husband, Thomas Michell, had bought the farm after he discovered that sometimes what you're looking for is right under your nose – at least it was when Thomas was prospecting for gold in the Cariboo. The gold wasn't quite under his nose; he found it under the corner of his cabin.

Thomas married Margaret Jenkins in 1856 and they made the 124 day voyage from Wales to Vancouver Island in 1862. They opened a grocery store on Johnson Street, and three years later Thomas left Margaret in charge of the store to go prospecting. He didn't find millions, but it was enough to come back to Victoria, sell the store, open the "What Cheer House" Inn on Yates Street and buy acreage in Saanich. Thomas bought 125 acres from Howard Estes, also purchasing his cattle, pigs, chickens, turkeys, wagon, plow and milking pans. Thomas also brought a basic knowledge of machinery to these primitive instruments, and bought the very first binder and steam-threshing machine to the Saanich Peninsula.

In many ways, the Michell's life was marked by tragedy. In addition to losing ten children, Margaret lost three brothers when they were relatively young: one was an officer of the Royal Navy who drowned on his first day of sea duty, and two others were professional singers who died from aneurisms.

Many of the surviving male children became farmers, and were among the first settlers of North Saanich. Some people call the Michell's the "backbone" of farming on the Saanich Peninsula, and many descendants are still active in the community. For example, one of the children, George Thomas, attended his first Saanichton fair as a baby and reportedly never missed the fall fair throughout his entire life. He also served as president of the North and South Agricultural Society and was honorary president when he died in 1963. Williard Michell, a grandson of Thomas and Margaret, had a dairy farm at 7421 East Saanich Road. He was a founding member and president of the Saanich Pioneer Society, a founding member of the Saanich Historical Artifacts Society, a past-president of the North and South Saanich Agricultural Society, and a founding member and past-president of Island Farms Dairy. Even when his health was failing, he continued to make day trips from the Saanich Peninsula Hospital to speak with students about pioneer days.

Ever since Margaret Michell rode sidesaddle to supervise another child's entrance into the world or visit an ailing citizen, the Michell family has been an invaluable part of the community.

Chatterton's Way

GEORGE CHATTERTON

George Louis Chatterton:
1916 - 1983

George Chatterton was born on a dairy farm in South Africa. He graduated with a degree in agriculture and briefly pursued graduate studies in animal genetics, but ultimately, he chose a career that had very little to do with any of these things. During his 67 years, George held many positions and jobs. He was an MP, a Saanich Reeve, a teacher and a door-to-door salesman. He was a member, director or president of more than ten community committees, boards, institutions and commissions, but, although he lived in Saanich for most of his adult life, he was never a farmer.

George was born in 1916 in Kimberley, South Africa, and graduated with a bachelor of science in agriculture from the University of Pretoria. After he completed his degree, he taught at an agricultural college in South Africa for a year before winning the prized Oliver

(Saanich Archives 1980-14-20)

Ash scholarship. The scholarship allowed him to enrol at any university in the world, and he chose to go to Cornell in Ithaca, N.Y. He took graduate studies in animal genetics, but his education was interrupted when the war broke out, and he never went back to finish.

George moved to Canada, and while he was waiting to be assigned a post by the Royal Canadian Air Force he worked as a door-to-door salesman, which was how he met his future wife, Kitty, in Ottawa. In 1942 he joined the Royal Canadian Air Force as a navigator. After the war, he married Kitty and they moved to Saanich. They bought a house at 500 Normandy Road and had four children, all of whom graduated from the University of Victoria.

When they first moved to Saanich, George worked for the federal government as the regional councillor for the Veterans' Land Act. It was the beginning of his political and community involvement.

In 1957 George was elected as a Saanich councillor, and the following year he was elected reeve in a by-election, a position he held for four years. In 1961, his political career expanded when George Pearkes, the Saanich-Esquimalt MP, was appointed Lieutenant-Governor, leaving the Conservatives with no candidate. George was approached by the local conservative group, and he had to make a difficult decision. At the time, George was working for the federal government and they considered it to be a conflict of interest for employees to run for candidacy, but they were not given a leave of absence, meaning George had to resign from his job before he was even nominated. Fortunately, he was nominated and served in the House of Commons from 1961 to 1968.

His community work included a term as president of the Parent-Teacher Association, a term as president of the Vancouver Island Municipalities Association and Chairman of the Saanich Police Board. He was also President of the Victoria chapter Appraisal Institute of Canada, was an executive member of the Agricultural Institute of Canada and spent two years on the Capital Region Planning Board of B.C.

In 1983, a street off Royal Oak Avenue was named Chatterton Way in order to celebrate the former reeve's numerous and varied contributions to the community of Saanich.

This biography has been sponsored by
Ida Chong, MLA
Oak Bay-Gordon Head
223 – 3930 Shelbourne Street, Victoria, BC V8P 5P6   Phone: 473-8528

The Strawberry & Daffodil Kings of Gordon Head

THE VANTREIGHT FAMILY

Geoffrey Vantreight Senior, Maud Bartholomew Vantreight,
Margaret and Helen (Saanich Archives 1984-12-15)

John Vantreight: 1844 - 1896
Florence Vantreight: 1858 – 1937

Geoffrey Arthur Vantreight: 1880 - 1959
Maude Bartholomew: 1898 – 1940

Geoffrey Arthur John Vantreight: 1924 – 2000
Jean Beckwith: 1923 –

When he stood on the porch of his big house on Tyndall Avenue in Gordon Head surveying his realm, Geoffrey Vantreight Sr. might have looked like a king, except that he wore Stanfield underwear with braces to hold up his weathered pants, and a tattered fedora on his head. It was a misleading image, and one that may have concealed the successful entrepreneur, businessman and politician that he was.

Geoffrey Vantreight, the "Strawberry King," served as a Saanich councillor and alderman, and worked every day to build a successful business on the land that he inherited from his father. He would pass the land on to his son, Geoff Jr, and from Geoff Jr. it would go to his sons. The Vantreight dynasty began when Geoffrey's parents, John and Florence, left Ireland. They moved to escape the unhappy memories of the place where their oldest child died of scarlet fever. They settled in Gordon Head in 1884 and paid $2 an acre for 135 acres of prime waterfront.

John had been a civil engineer for the Irish government, and he was involved in the formation of many roads in Gordon Head, and frequently made the seven-mile walk to the legislature buildings to petition for new roads and a school.

His petitions were ultimately successful; a small one-room schoolhouse was established at the corners of Tyndall and Grandview, and Gordon Head Elementary will celebrate its 115th anniversary in 2006.

When John died in 1896, Geoffrey was only 16-years-old, but as the oldest son he was the only one who could run the farm. The headstrong teenager quickly adapted a routine of rising at 4 a.m., demanding that his sisters rise equally early to cook him a beef-steak breakfast (he refused to eat eggs.) He eventually decided to move the Gordon Head farm. He bought 20 acres on Tyndall Avenue for its superior soil, and in 1906 he and his younger brothers moved into a small shack on the property, while his mother and sisters moved into the city.

In 1914, Geoffrey married Maude Bartholomew. Shortly after, they moved into a small house built by the carpenter in the family, Sydney. Although Geoffrey didn't like to spend money, the apple crop in the 1920's was so profitable he decided it was time to move to a larger house. The house, at 4423 Tyndall Avenue, is still family-owned. Geoffrey Sr. enjoyed considerable success in berry farming, but he never fully explored the possibilities of flower farming. In 1913 Geoffrey Sr. persuaded his neighbour, William Edwards, who was a recent immigrant from the Scilly Isles, to part with some of his daffodil bulbs, but

Geoffrey Vantreight Senior
(Saanich Archives 1984-12-23)

it was left up to Geoff Jr. to turn the eventual flowers into a profit. Geoff Jr. made them his project in the 1940's and 1950's, and it became so successful that he earned a title as illustrious as his father's – he became the Daffodil King, and was soon shipping bulbs and flowers across Canada and around the world.

In 1956, Geoff sold his first batch of daffodils to the Cancer Society to promote their annual cancer drive. Three years later, he was their largest supplier. Today, the daffodil has become a symbol of hope for all those suffering from cancer; millions of Vantreight daffodils were shipped to all parts of Canada and across the border.

Geoff Jr. married Jean Beckwith in 1945 and they had seven children. Today, pioneer John Vantreight's great-grandsons, Ian and Michael, own and manage G.A. Vantreight and Sons. The 750-acre empire of fruit, vegetables and flowers is currently facing an uncertain future: in August of 2005, a court order stated that the business differences between the brothers required that the property be sold, with either brother having the option to buy it. Temperamental weather, fluctuating markets and a land-hungry society have always made farming an uncertain business, but the Vantreights have been in the business for over 120 years, and show every intention of maintaining the family dynasty.

Bringing the Modern World to Saanich

FRANK COPLEY

Basil Oldfield, Frank Copley, Claude Butler (L to R), c1950s (Courtesy Guy Copley)

Frank Copley: 1913 – 1968

Years ago, when many businesses and workplaces were rife with prejudice and racism, the employment practises of Frank Malahat Judson Copley were remarkably enlightened. He hired youths who were experiencing problems either at home or at school. He gave many people their first jobs. He was one of the earliest contractors to hire workers who were not Caucasian, despite the disapproval of many of his employees, some of whom threatened to quit if Frank insisted on hiring them. Frank Jr. remembers his father telling his sons, "We will just see what happens," and hired them anyway.

Frank Copley was the oldest of four boys. His family owned and logged much of what is the Shawnigan Lake area today, until they were forced to sell most of it during the depression. Frank's brothers Guy and Theo joined the military, and Frank and Norm began a trucking and excavating business. Guy spent 32 years with the Navy, while Theo left the military at the end of the war and worked as an equipment operator with Frank and Norm, whose business had taken off. They had started by hauling wood from the Prospect Lake area to the greenhouses on Shelbourne Street; they also hauled bark from their father's property in Shawnigan with a Reo Speed wagon.

The Copley brothers introduced bulldozers and mechanical shovels to road construction and excavation projects. Their equipment replaced the horse drawn road equipment that had been used in Saanich and Greater Victoria. They convinced many contractors to switch to a mechanized system, and the increased speed with which they could complete jobs meant there was no shortage of business. They branched out and bought top-quality bulldozers, shovels, grader equipment and heavy trucks.

Eventually, Frank and Norm split up the company. Norm took operations from Bamberton north and Frank took lower Vancouver Island. In 1952, Frank and his wife Bea bought 120 acres on Carey Road for $25,000. Today, most of this property is Northridge subdivision. An avid flyer, Frank built a 1500 by 200 foot airstrip on which he flew his four-seat Stinson Voyager, one of three planes he owned during his lifetime. He served as President of the Victoria Flying Club for three years and was director for many more. He was also involved in building a strip on what is now UVic property; he and Claude Butler made the only landing and takeoff from that particular field, as the DOT refused to license it. It seems the neighbours were less thrilled about the prospect of a UVic airstrip than the pilots. Instead, DOT allowed for two radio towers to be installed on the property.

In the 1950's, Frank Copley wasn't the only owner of a private airstrip. Claude Butler owned a strip off of Keating Road, near Butlers pit, and still exists today. Joe Howroyd had a strip on his property at Shelbourne and Mortimer Streets. Quite often, Frank Copley and his family would hop in his plane and travel to one of the other local strips, or make a trip up island.

Frank had two sons, Frank Jr. and Robert. Their father taught his children to respect people regardless of their race, religious beliefs or station in life, and he was always especially proud when any of his employees went on to be successful in their own business. When Frank Jr. graduated from Mount View High School, his father hosted

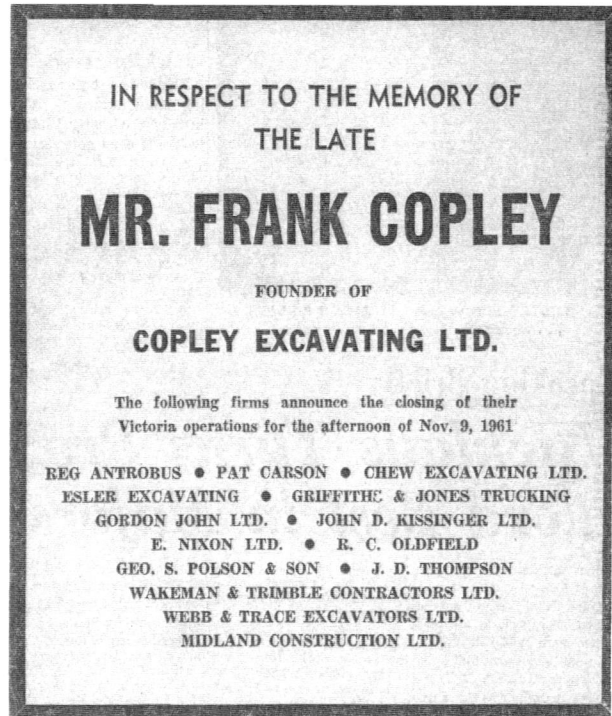

IN RESPECT TO THE MEMORY OF
THE LATE

MR. FRANK COPLEY

FOUNDER OF

COPLEY EXCAVATING LTD.

The following firms announce the closing of their
Victoria operations for the afternoon of Nov. 9, 1961

REG ANTROBUS ● PAT CARSON ● CHEW EXCAVATING LTD.
ESLER EXCAVATING ● GRIFFITHS & JONES TRUCKING
GORDON JOHN LTD. ● JOHN D. KISSINGER LTD.
E. NIXON LTD. ● R. C. OLDFIELD
GEO. S. POLSON & SON ● J. D. THOMPSON
WAKEMAN & TRIMBLE CONTRACTORS LTD.
WEBB & TRACE EXCAVATORS LTD.
MIDLAND CONSTRUCTION LTD.

(Courtesy Guy Copley)

a grad party for the entire graduating class on the family's Carey Road property. Everyone was welcome to dance, talk, have breakfast and swim in the pool, but Frank stipulated that there was to be absolutely no alcohol. He discretely screened guests as they arrived, and by many accounts, the first Dry Grad in the area was a huge success.

When Frank died suddenly in 1961 at 48, most of the construction and excavation companies on lower Vancouver Island closed down for the day so the employees could attend his service. It was a prime example of the great esteem with which Frank was held in the community.

This biography has been sponsored by

Copley Bros. Construction Ltd.
4760 Beaverdale Road, Victoria, BC   V8Z 6K2   (250) 479-4151

Gordon Head Recreation Centre under construction (Saanich Archives 1981-21-12)

1966 - 1975

Saanich residents during the 1960s and 1970s must have become accustomed to the sounds of construction all around them. The celebrations for Canada's centennial in 1967 kicked off with the building of Centennial Stadium at UVIC. G.R. Pearkes arena, the Senior Citizen Activity Centre at Hampton Park, Gordon Head Recreation Centre, Lambrick park and Cedar Hill Community Centre all followed in rapid succession. The area from Pat Bay to Quadra Street was reconstructed, and a new highway was built from Quadra Street to Finnerty Road, named for pioneer Kenneth McKenzie. The public beaches at Elk and Beaver Lakes expanded, and Cedar Hill Golf Course transferred from private to municipal control and has since become one of the busiest municipal courses in Canada.

In 1969 the age of technology dawned and Saanich used its first computer for data processing. Development continued both at the UVIC campus, which was granted its own fire station in 1974; and the Lansdowne campus, which merged with the B.C. Vocational School on Interurban, became Camosun College in 1970.

An Amateur Astronomer

GEORGE BALL

George Ball

When George Ball said he liked to look at the stars from his backyard, he didn't just mean while relaxing in a lawn chair. The observatory he constructed in his former backyard in the Gorge-Burnside area contained a 12.5-inch Schmidt Cassegrain, a 6-inch Schmidt Cassegrain and numerous other instruments all mounted on an enormous German Equatorial Mount. Even for those not in-the-know on astronomical equipment, it's clear that George is serious about the stars.

Even more impressive than his collection of equipment is that George designed and built all his telescopes in his basement workshop. That doesn't just mean assembling the pieces, either. George completed every step, from grinding and

Dominion Astrophysical Observatory (Saanich Archives 1993-1-20)

aluminizing his own mirrors to mounting all the apparatus.

His passion for building equipment stems from his father, John Thomas Ball, who won the Best Set in Show award at the 1925 Victoria Radio Show. John Ball had emigrated to Canada in 1905, first operating a small business in Napina, Manitoba before moving to Victoria where he opened the first electrical business of its kind on Harriet Road. George joined his father's business in 1925, and by 1946, Ball Electric was installing two-way FM radio sets in the Saanich police and Fire department vehicles. George took over the business in 1945, moved it to a new location at the corner of Burnside and Harriet, and was joined by partner Howard Shemilt in 1951. His late wife Rose was an enormous help to George during these busy years, and the couple raised two daughters in Saanich.

After retirement, George's passion turned from radios to telescopes, and he has amassed quite a collection. His projects often incorporated some unique and unusual features. Take his dome-shaped observatory for example: instead of having the usual rotating dome, his entire observatory rotated on a circular track. The telescope inside moved along either axis on a motor George could control from his cushioned chair—equipped with a crank so he could raise or lower himself to the eyepiece.

All this work required much time and talent, but that never stood in George's way. He joined the Victoria Centre of the Royal Astronomical Society of Canada in 1955, and was on the council a year later. He soon became a representative to the National Council, and served as Vice President of the Victoria centre, Director of Telescopes and Observations, and National Coordinator for Instrumentation.

As George became well-known for his superb instruments, others came to him for help and advice, which he was always happy to share. He used his own equipment to aluminize mirrors for other amateur astronomers, and assisted others in the construction of their own telescopes. For years, he hosted public observation nights, arranged for displays at hobby shows and assisted at the Dominion Astronomical Observatory on public evenings. George was awarded the Royal Astronomical Society's Service Award in 1968. In April of 2004, he generously donated his observatory and equipment to the Victoria Centre of the Royal Astronomical Society. To accomplish the move, a crane threaded the dome between power wires and hedges. The equipment is a legacy for future astronomers that also includes his well-kept historical records and the respected Newton-Ball Award.

Doris Page at the dedication of the Doris Page Winter Garden, The Horticulture Centre, 1985
(Courtesy The Horticulture Centre)

For the Love of Plants

DORIS PAGE

Doris Page: 1914 - 1999

The Doris Page Winter Garden contains over 500 different species of plants, shrubs and trees, and at any time of the year, some of these plants will provide a colourful and vibrant display. Whether it's snowdrops blooming in January and February, winter irises, or Chinese witch-hazel

and Cornelian cherry that offer colour year-round, visitors will always have something to see at the Winter Garden.

The garden was established in 1985 by the Horticultural Centre of the Pacific, and named in honour of Doris Page for her many years of work demonstrating the potential for winter gardens in climates like Vancouver Island. Doris was actively involved in planning the garden, even though she had to use a walker to navigate the paths and slopes of the property. The woman herself is considered a pioneer of winter and naturalistic gardening in the Pacific Northwest, and the Doris Page Winter Garden is one of the few of its kind.

Doris was born in Barrow-in-Furness, Lancashire, on December 9, 1914. She graduated from a three-year course in horticulture from Sudley College in 1935 and worked as a horticulturist in the U.K. and Tanganyika before immigrating to Canada in 1948.

Shortly after Doris arrived in Canada, she began working for Ed Lohbrunner at Lakeview Garden Nursery off Blenkinsop Road. She worked at the Lakeview Nursery for 32 years.

Doris was a prominent name in horticultural society. She was twice elected president of the Victoria Horticultural Society, and was involved with the Rock and Alpine Society and the Thetis Park Nature Sanctuary. Many people may recognize her name from her television show. From 1973 - 1991 she hosted the weekly show "Island Country Garden" on CHEK Channel 6 Victoria. For 18 years, Doris gave helpful garden tips and information to viewers.

Doris lived in a 1920's cottage at the corner of Haliburton Road and Lochside Drive. The land - eight-tenths of an acre - had attracted Doris because of its plentiful dogwood trees and other native plants and shrubs. Her friends often said that Doris considered the outdoors to be more important than the indoors.

Doris's love of plants also manifested itself as a desire for conservation, and her actions led to a sizeable piece of land in Saanich being saved from development.

The land across from Doris's cottage was an 88-hectare property called Tank Park or Cordova Bay Park, and, while wild land, was not officially designated as a park. When there were murmurs that it was planned to turn it into a housing development, Doris collected 200 signatures in protest, and went to speak to Saanich council. She insisted that council check the property title, and when they did, they discovered that half of the land had been donated in 1919 by Roy Irvine, the son of Jack "Long Gun" Irvine - and it was bequeathed to Saanich on the condition that it remain a park. In response, Saanich council officially made the land a park, and in January of 1990, named a portion of it "Doris Page Park" in recognition of her horticultural contributions. Fittingly, she also bequeathed her eight-tenths of an acre to Saanich as parkland when she died.

The Doris Page Winter Garden at the Horticulture Centre continues to be maintained by volunteers and funds from the Doris Page Memorial Fund. In fact, in 2000, the garden was upgraded and expanded, ensuring that Doris' goal of showing the beauty of winter gardens will continue through the decades.

This biography has been sponsored by
The Horticulture Centre

The Dobber

KEN DOBSON

Ken "Dobber" Dobson: – 1995

It's probably safe to say that hockey players in Canada are the most revered sports figures in the country. During hockey season, go to any bar or restaurant with a television in Victoria and chances are that you will see a hockey game. Chances are equally good that the hockey fans in the audience will know most of the players and the coaches. But often the announcers and commentators, the people who give a voice to the game and offer their excitement, passion and knowledge to their thousands of viewers and listeners, go nameless.

Ken Dobson, however, was not one to go unnoticed. Called brutally honest, an irascible rascal, and the five-foot-two-inch man with the eight-foot-six voice, "Dobber" was the sports director at C-FAX Radio for 20 years. In the course of his career, he covered many important sporting events, including the 1972 Canada-Russia hockey series and the National Fastball Championships in Victoria in 1983. In

(Courtesy C-FAX)

1994, he became one of only 10 people to be inducted into the International Hockey Hall of Fame in the "Media and Friends Category" for his contribution to the growth and development of hockey.

Dobber was well known in Saanich as the Santa Claus on Candy Cane Lane, otherwise known as Tattersal Drive, where he lived with his wife May and their three children. Every year the Dobber would don the red suit to hand out candy to the children who came to see the Christmas lights. He was probably well suited to that Santa outfit, since most of his friends say Dobber had a "magnificent attitude" and always made people smile. In fact, when he was negotiating with an author to write his autobiography, they ran into difficulties because the writer wanted to write a serious book, and seriousness ran entirely contrary to Dobber.

Dobber was born in Hamilton, Ontario in 1923. He served in the Royal Canadian Air

Force in the Second World War as a Leading Aircraftsman, which lead him to believe his talents would suit broadcasting. From 1946 to 1975 he worked for several different radio and television stations in both announcer and manager positions. In 1975 Victoria's C-FAX approached him, and there Dobber remained until retirement. Over the years, Dobber became a face as much as a voice for sport in Victoria. He received hundreds of letters and plaques from sports clubs and other community groups thanking him for his various community services. In 1993 he was named an honorary firefighter.

Included in his legacy is an annual scholarship worth over $1,000 awarded to a Grade 12 student who shows exemplary participation in community or athletic activities. There is also the "Ken Dobson Memorial Award," which awards $1500 to the best overall poster created by a student for the Burn Fund Poster Contest.

When Ken Dobson died in 1995 after two and a half years of living with cancer, more than 1500 people attended the Memorial Arena to honour his memory. The city named the press box at the arena "Dobber's Den," and the hour-long ceremony was broadcast on C-FAX.

When Dobber decided that he would make a good broadcaster, he showed extraordinary insight. On the airwaves, in the press box or wearing a Santa Claus suit, Ken Dobson had a lasting influence on the community that people will remember even in the absence of his daily broadcasts.

This biography has been sponsored by

The Gowards of Goward House
THE GOWARD FAMILY

Elizabeth and Owen Goward, 1938 (Courtesy Bernard Goward)

Elizabeth Goward: 1910 – 2002
Owen Goward: 1906 – 1983

When it came to painting, Elizabeth and Owen Goward encountered obstacles far more often than they found inspiration. Owen's father suffered a stroke when Owen was only seven years old, which meant he was financially responsible at a young age and had no opportunity to seriously study painting. Elizabeth was born into a wealthy family and graduated from the Art Institute of Philadelphia, only to experience the necessity of working in a bank to support her family during the depression.

Though neither of them achieved critical acclaim, they both continued to paint throughout very busy lives: Elizabeth spent her lunch hours in the vault, painting the portraits of other bank employees, and also taught art lessons. In his off-time, Owen painted the landscapes of Oregon and B.C.

Owen grew up in Cadboro Bay, graduated from Oak Bay high school and attended a two-year program at Craigdarroch College before setting out for Astoria, Oregon. He joined a survey team and completed an engineering course through correspondence, and was soon placed in charge of the crew.

Owen and Elizabeth met in Saanich while they were both on holidays; Owen from his job in Oregon and Elizabeth from her home in Philadelphia. They were married in 1938 and settled in Gearhart, Oregon. Meanwhile, Elizabeth faced a conundrum. While she wanted to dedicate her life to her family, people so often requested her portrait services – she was particularly adept at capturing the likeness of children – that she was soon exhausted.

During the war, Owen worked as a logging engineer, while Elizabeth "drifted into a life of pleasure-seeking with no depth or meaning," according to an Islander article. Then her daughter Mary suffered severe burns when her clothing caught fire. Mary survived, but the episode scared Elizabeth and inspired her to join the Moral Re-armament group, which lead to the illustration of a book titled *Listen to the Children*.

When the war ended, the Gowards returned to Cadboro Bay to take over the family home built in 1908 at 2495 Arbutus Road. Elizabeth held art classes on the second storey, and the students, many of them elderly women, had to climb a skinny ladder while holding their cumbersome easels and paint boxes.

Owen was active in the B.C. forest industry and protested against the slash and burn forestry practices employed by the province. He also served as a consultant engineer for 37 years, spending more than half his married life away from his wife and five children.

Owen suffered the first of three heart attacks in 1959, and he decided to use his convalescence time to open an art gallery in his home. He printed hundreds of brochures and posters announcing the event, only to be summoned back to work just four months after his heart attack. The Goward Gallery was not opened until after Owen's retirement in 1971, when he also began to hold shows in Victoria, Vancouver and Kelowna.

In 1973, the Gowards sold the house to Saanich because they were unable to keep paying taxes on the estate without subdividing, which Owen refused to do, but they retained a lifetime occupancy of the property.

In 1991 the historic house underwent a $440,000 renovation headed by the Goward House Society to turn it into a seniors centre, a community hall, and most appropriately, as an art gallery that showcases local artists.

Goward House, Arbutus Road (Saanich Archives 1982-13-24)

This biography has been sponsored by

VICTORIA CHAMBER OF COMMERCE
850 Courtney Street, Victoria, BC V8W 1C4   (250) 383-7191

St Joseph's Hospital (Courtesy Barry F. King)

A Pioneering Back Surgeon

FOUAD HAMDI

Fouad Ahmed Hamdi: 1922 – 2003

Though his own career was cut short by a debilitating illness, Dr. Hamdi made great contributions to the field of medicine. For many years, he was the only neurosurgeon on Vancouver Island. He was considered a world leader in back surgery. He also played an important role in the establishment of a neuropsychology laboratory at the Royal Jubilee Hospital.

Dr. Hamdi was born in Alexandria, Egypt in 1922. He was from a large family, and it was mainly through scholarships that he was able to obtain two doctorates from the University of Edinburgh, one in neurosurgery and one in ophthalmology in 1951.

He lived in both London and South Wales and met his wife Julia, a nurse, in England. They would have two sons, Ramsay and Llew, and a daughter, Rhiannon. After the war, they emigrated to Canada, first settling in Saskatoon and later Regina. They moved to Victoria in 1962, where Dr. Hamdi worked at both St. Joseph's hospital and the Royal Jubilee Hospital. Since he was the only neurosurgeon and was working before there were seat belts or helmets, the job was often both long and physically and mentally draining.

Dr. Hamdi made medical history when he successfully inserted the first artificial (stainless steel) vertebra into William Hamilton on August 2, 1968. He would complete three more successful transplants before he retired. The procedure was intended for patients whose bones were collapsing from cancer, and helped them maintain their mobility, even preventing paralysis. He also devised an artificial disc in partnership with the Kena Metal Company. He was presented to the legislature in 1968, and made an Honorary Citizen of the City of Victoria in 1971.

Tragically, in 1976, he was afflicted with a debilitating illness (polycythemia) that would make it impossible for him to stand for long hours at the operating table. Among other things, this disease causes an increase in the manufacture of red blood cells, which brings a plethora of problems, including pain. He was forced to retire at age 54, but even then he didn't retire his surgery skills. An avid bird lover, Hamdi turned his skills to operating on the winged variety of species, who were brought to him by an animal care worker.

He was also involved in the establishment of the neuropsychology department at UVic and he sat on its board of directors. Dr. William Gaddes, a professor in the psychology department at UVic, worked closely with Dr. Hamdi towards the establishment of neuropsychology labs at Royal Jubilee Hospital and the University.

Dr. Hamdi was interested in research projects at the University, while Gaddes was looking to establish a research relationship with neurosurgery. After several initial trial clinics, Dr. Hamdi successfully petitioned the hospital board for permanent space for the Neuropsychology Laboratory, so that in-patients could be tested at short notice, and neuropsychological diagnostic services became a regular service at the hospital. According to Gaddes' memoir, this was the first neuropsychology laboratory in any hospital in B.C. The Jubilee lab was established in 1965 and Vancouver followed with a similar service in its hospitals a few years later.

As a talented and dedicated surgeon, Dr. Hamdi's work touched the lives of countless numbers of patients, students, members of the medical community and, later in his career, his feathered friends.

The King of Comedy
COLIN SKINNER

Colin Skinner: d. 2003

When Colin Skinner was four years old, he developed a high fever while ill with the German Measles. It affected his hearing, which gradually diminished until he was almost completely deaf by the time he was a teenager. Nevertheless, he received good marks in school, but by the time he became a teacher years later, he realized how poor his hearing was and began to use a hearing aid.

But his ears never hampered his teaching or his acting career. They may, in fact, have helped him, since much of Colin's route to becoming the "King of Comedy" was marked by a series of coincidences connected to his hearing problem. Colin won a scholarship to the Teachers' College in Kirksville, Missouri, but his parents couldn't afford to send him overseas. When the headline, "poor deaf boy receives U.S. Scholarship," ran in the London Evening News, an American philanthropist volunteered to pay Colin's expenses. When he arrived in the U.S., two more American benefactors stepped in: one was a Presbyterian minister who gave Skinner a place to stay during vacations, and the other was a Florida businessman who paid Skinner's living expenses. Without the newspaper headline, Colin may never have come to North America.

After graduation, Colin taught for four years in Missouri before moving

(Courtesy St. Michaels University School, Archives)

to Vancouver Island. His decision to come to the Island was random – he had a pupil who had an aunt in Nanaimo, which he thought was a pretty name. His first job was with St. Michaels University School. He taught there for three years before he began working towards an MA in English at UVic. When the UVic drama teacher asked him if he could do a Cockney accent, it led to the role of Aborson, the executioner in *Measure of Measure*, which in turn led to a career shift.

Colin abandoned his English studies and graduated with an MFA in Theatre in 1969. To get around his hearing impairment, he developed techniques, such as using the shutting of a door to make a vibration instead of relying on a line for a cue. As well as teaching drama at SMUS and Glenlyon Schools, he became known as the "farce King" as he directed, produced and starred in many revivals of British sex farce comedies put on at the McPherson Playhouse.

Among Colin's protégés were Atom Egoyan, now a famous Canadian film director, and Andrew Sabiston and Tim Williams, the co-creators of the musical stage production *Napoleon*.

Colin has also had his share of bad reviews.

In the play *Cash on Delivery,* one character pretends to have Tourette's Syndrome, and while many reviewers thought the spoof of Tourette's was hilarious, some people felt it was cruel. And in another Capital Comedy play, one actor appeared entirely naked – although it wasn't Colin, who always played his roles knowing that the next day he would be facing a classroom of teenagers.

In his 26 years at SMUS, Colin developed the drama program from a single annual school play to a programme of four full productions, with up to 220 students involved in each. He also met his second wife, Margaret, a mathematician and musician, at St. Michaels.

When Colin died of cancer at age 67, a most appropriate tribute was held for Victoria's "Clown Prince of Comedy" at the McPherson Playhouse. The program featured many well-known actors, musicians, dancers and singers. Donations for the event went towards establishing a scholarship in Colin's name, perhaps the best way to ensure his crown is passed on to another talented king.

This biography has been sponsored by

Paul Bishop

Pay Less, Give More

ALLEN VANDEKERKHOVE

(Courtesy Times Colonist)

Allen Vandekerkhove: 1937 –

Many years ago, the Halloween-orange insignia of Pay Less Gas Stations were a common sight on Vancouver Island. While Pay Less was bought by Shell Canada almost two decades ago, many people will still remember its former owner, Allen Vandekerkhove, for the regular gas price wars he waged against larger companies. He continually offered gas at a significantly lower price than Shell and Petro-Canada, and also gave out "pay less coupons" to encourage customers to come to Pay Less.

Allen's history in the gas business had slow beginnings, but when the company was sold to Shell Canada in 1989 for a reported $40 million, Pay Less had 52 stations on Vancouver Island and gross sales of more than $100 million.

In 1972, the propane company that Allen worked for wanted to transfer him to Montreal, where they felt his bilingual skills would be better utilized. But Allen didn't want to go – instead, he left his job and bought two gas stations on Goldstream and Sooke Roads from Bill Koelmell. Eighteen months later, he bought two more stations, this time at Duncan and Cassidy. But none of them was doing particularly well, and Allen was becoming discouraged. Then, his old employer from the propane company phoned and offered to buy out all the stations if Allen would agree to go to Montreal. Far from feeling tempted to accept the offer, it provided the extra incentive Allen needed to make the business a success.

He converted a car wash into a pump station on leased property on Tillicum and Burnside Roads, and it quickly became the best station in sales, generating more revenue than the other four combined. Even the coin operated vacuum cleaner was bringing in $1,000 a month.

Allen lives in a ranch house on 100 acres in Saanich. A pair of horses rear up on the gable-end of the house outlined in contrasting colours of stone. Now that Allen has finished fighting the gas war with Petro-Canada and Shell, he's gone back to his roots by taking up hobby farming, although the heavy-duty mower, raker, baler and stacker he uses to produce 4,000 to 5,000 bales of hay a season belie the word "hobby," and suggest that Allen pursues his hobbies with the same verve and determination he showed when running a business.

Allen was born in Iles des Chenes, Manitoba. He had farming in his background; when he used to visit his grandmother as a six-year-old, she would put him to work milking the cows. From there, he progressed to driving a tractor, the farm combine and trucks. When he was 13-years-old, he got his drivers license (he may have been helped here by his mother's cousin, who ran the licensing office for the town.)

He has been married to his wife Loreen for over 50 years and they have six children. Both have been involved in numerous charities, including multiple United Way Campaigns and the Victoria Hospice Society fundraisers. The Vandekerkhove family also initiated the Vandekerkhove Foundation, which supports numerous community events and charities and has donated more than $500,000 annually since 1985. The foundation donated $1 million dollars to establish the Centre of Studies in Religion and Society at UVic, and the university renamed the Sedgewick Building's B-wing the Allen and Loreen Vandekerkhove Wing in their honour. They have both received honorary degrees from UVic; Allen in 1990 and Loreen in 2002.

Many people probably wish that Allen Vandekerkhove was still offering Pay Less coupons and providing incentive to other companies to keep prices lower.

The Quintessential Canadian

AL PURDY

Al Purdy: 1919 – 2000

"This guy's not a poet. He looks like a boom man from my dad's logging camp," said Al Purdy's publisher, Howard White, when he met Purdy for the first time. He also said Purdy "used slang and talked like an ordinary person," a trait that would contribute to him being called the quintessential Canadian, and a man who was at the forefront of a poetry revolution.

Purdy wrote about hockey games and fighting with the foreman at work. He made poetry available to a broader audience, to "ordinary" people who appreciated his subject matter and his straightforward manner.

Many people criticized Purdy for his colloquial style, average subject matter, unpretentious language and apparent simplicity of his work. But he often tackled themes as complex as the endurance of art and its ability to transcend death, and issues as varied as the rugged Canadian landscape and its characters.

Purdy wasn't only a poet for the amateur reader, either. He won several prestigious Canadian awards, including the Governor General's Award for *The Cariboo Horses* in 1966 and a second time for *Collected poems, 1956 – 1986*, in 1986. In 1983, he was inducted into the Order of Canada.

Purdy's level of success was all the more remarkable considering that he came from an uninspired background. He was a high school dropout who freely admitted that his first book was "atrocious." It wasn't until he turned 40 that he started to write seriously and achieved a small

(Courtesy Saanich News)

measure of success. Before then, he worked at a variety of manual jobs. During the Depression he rode the rails to Vancouver. He served with the RCAF during the war, and according to White, he "got in at the lowest rung and was demoted from there."

Purdy supported himself at labour jobs and posing for art classes before his freelance writing, book reviews and volumes of poetry began to generate income, though it never made him rich.

As the voice of the common person, he was extremely successful, but some people suggested that his poetry was partly responsible for the dumbing-down of language. In one infamous article that sparked outrage from readers across the country, the National Post published a piece that stated bluntly, "The voice of the common man is not the voice of poetry," and that Purdy was "the apotheosis of eh".

But Purdy was just as aware of his deficiencies as any critic. He wrote a poem titled "On Realizing He Has Written Some Bad Poems," and on a separate occasion, included this line: "I have been stupid in a poem". His wife Eurithe, to whom he was married for more than 58 years, was frequently featured as the perfect foil to the foolish poet.

Purdy had a faithful following of readers, and when he died of lung cancer in his Lochside home in 2000, the many memorials and tributes made to him were an acknowledgment of the effect his work had on the Canadian psyche. When the "Poetry In Transit Effort" was introduced to public buses in Victoria, Purdy's work received a special tribute, so that Canada's poet would continue to influence readers, and his art, as prophesized in his own poem, would transcend his own passing.

Moving Dodd House to Lambrick Park, 1978 (Saanich Archives 1980-1-1)

1976 - 1985

A step in preserving the rural heritage of Saanich was taken when structures such as Tolmie School, Cedar Hill Elementary, Braefoot Annex, Captain Dodd House, Victoria Normal School, Strawberry Vale School, Royal Oak Elementary, Wilkinson Road Jail and the Dominion Astrophysical Observatory were designated as Heritage sites. Rural development included the designation of the Blenkinsop Valley area for agricultural use in 1977 and the creation of a permanent nature centre at the Swan Lake Christmas Hill site. Urban development was also underway as Broadmead Farms was rezoned for a shopping centre. Firefighters were busy with the opening of Fire Hall 2, the initiation of their new DOT Locator program to assist in finding disabled or handicapped persons during a fire, and the implementation of a Water Rescue Service in cooperation with the Coast Guard. They also developed a self-propelled ATV boat trailer to enhance water rescue capabilities.

The house of Captain Charles and Grace Dodd, the oldest house still standing in Saanich, was moved from its original location at the northeast corner of Kenmore Road and Torquay Drive. The single-storey, cedar house, surrounded by a picket fence now stands at 4139 Lambrick Way.

Saanich showed its commitment to youth through the formation of a special youth council to combat rising delinquency and vandalism , and the building of a skateboard park on Finlayson street in 1982. Staff and citizens worked together on a neighbourhood improvement program in the Battleford area, and the municipality purchased King's Pond, now a Wildlife Sanctuary. The municipality adopted a Coat of Arms in 1981, a symbol of life in Saanich still in use today. Its green shield represents the soil of the land, and the farmer, plough and trees remind residents of the farming and logging history of Saanich. "Populo Serviendo," the Latin motto inscribed along the bottom means "Serving the People."

Putting the Ball in the Net

NORM BAKER

(Courtesy Nancy Baker)

Norm Baker: 1912-1989

As a sixteen year old, Norm Baker became the youngest player to be part of a Senior National Championship team when the Victoria Dominoes won the Canadian Basketball Championship in 1939.

Professional basketball was a different game then, with little of the spinning, dunking and acrobatics fans are accustomed to seeing on the court today. When Norm played, pushing and elbowing to jockey for position was standard, and that suited Norm—as a burly 6'2" player, he had the build to dominate under the net and the finesse to make it look easy. Abe Saperstein, former manager of the Harlem Globetrotters described him as, "one of the greatest natural basketball players [he had] ever seen". Basketball wasn't the only sport Norm was a natural at, either. As a youngster growing up a few blocks from Victoria High on Camosun Street, he also played soccer, baseball, and lacrosse.

The bombing of Pearl Harbour in 1941 enticed Norm and his older brother Ralph, who resides in Saanich, to join the Canadian Air Force as airplane mechanics. The two trained south of London, Ontario, and were then posted close to home at the Patricia Bay base until 1945. Throughout his service, basketball remained a focus of Norm's life. He led the Pat Bay Royal Canadian Air Force Club Gremlins to a championship in 1943, scoring a record 38 points in a single game. Ralph played on the same line as his younger brother, and remembers Norm's dominance on the court. "When Norm and I were playing together," he says with a laugh, "he'd get a smile on his face and I'd know someone was going to get hammered".

After leading the Dominoes to two more Canadian Championships in 1942 and 1946, Norm turned professional and moved south to play for the Chicago Stags. He returned to Canada for two seasons with the Vancouver Hornets from 1947 to 1948, scoring 1962 points in only 70 games. Between basketball seasons, Norm excelled at lacrosse, and was named a top-ten scorer in the Western Lacrosse Association in 1949 as a member of the New Westminster Adanacs. His son, Norm Jr. would repeat this accomplishment with the Victoria Shamrocks 29 years later.

Norm returned to the U.S.A in 1949 to play basketball for the Boston Celtics. During a memorable game that season against the Globetrotters, Norm scored 39 points in the first half. A year later, he played for the Boston Whirlwinds, where he stayed for three seasons. That year, Norm was named Canadian Basketball Player of the Half-Century, and was the only non-American player chosen for the Stars of the World team that toured Europe.

The professional basketball league in the early 1950s was markedly smaller than the NBA today, giving players the opportunity to become friends as well as opponents. When the Harlem Globetrotters movie was filming in 1950, the team invited Norm's fiancé Nancy to Hollywood to watch some of the taping. Norm can be spotted wearing number 16 in some of the game footage shown in the movie.

When Norm retired from professional basketball in 1953,

he returned home to work as a Police Officer in Saanich from 1954 to 1975. He shared his love of sports by coaching basketball and lacrosse. Recognition of Norm's athletic accomplishments came when he was inducted into the B.C. Sports Hall of Fame in 1966, into the Canadian Sports Hall of Fame in 1978, and into the Canadian Basketball Hall of Fame in 1979. A skilled lacrosse player and basketball star , Norm Baker is one of the strongest athletes to come out of B.C.

(Courtesy Ralph Baker)

This biography has been sponsored by

RECREATION

Saanich Recreation (250) 475-5422
www.saanichrecreation.ca

Ken and Kathy Shields, c1980 (Courtesy UVic Archives 0081130818)

The Royal Couple of Roundball

KEN & KATHY SHIELDS

Kathy Shields: 1951 –

Ken Shields: 1946 –

Between them, Ken and Kathy Shields have collected 15 national titles coaching the University of Victoria's men's and women's basketball teams. They have both been national team coaches, leading Canada to Olympic qualifiers and several world championships. Even their Airedale terrier is named "Koach." The Sheilds' passion for the game and support for each other has helped them achieve some of the greatest honours possible in Canadian basketball.

The athletic duo met at the University of British Columbia (UBC), when Ken was a co-mentor and Kathy was a 5-foot-9 forward on team Thunderbird. With Mr. Basketball coaching and the future Mrs. Basketball playing, UBC won the Canadian championship in 1969.

Ken left the T-Birds in 1971 and moved to Sudbury, Ontario, to coach the men's team at Laurentian University. Kathy moved there a year later to complete her Bachelor of Commerce degree in sports administration, and won two more Canadian Intercollegiate Athletic Union (CIAU) titles in 1974 and 1975 with the Laurentian team. In 1976, Ken and Kathy married, and by 1978 they were back in B.C. and Ken coaching the men's basketball team at UVic. Meanwhile, Kathy was dealing with a back injury that was making it harder and harder to play, until finally it took her off the basketball court and put her into a full-body cast. No longer able to play basketball, Ken pushed Kathy towards coaching and encouraged her to take the junior varsity coach position at UVic, when the women's team was still called the "Vikettes."

Both of the Shields' careers flourished at UVic. During Ken's tenure as the UVic head coach from 1978 to 1989, the Vikes won an amazing seven-year streak of CIAU titles – a record Kathy surpassed in 2000 when she won eight titles. Kathy, who was also the national coach from 1993 to 1995, and was named Coach of the Year in 2000. After more than two decades of coaching at UVic, Kathy acquired eight Canadian Interuniversity Sport (CIS) national and 14 Canadian West championships, and compiled a regular season record of 320 wins against 50 losses in 370 games.

In 1998, Ken was inducted into the Order of Canada, and many consider him to be the most successful coach in the history of Canadian university basketball. Both Ken and Kathy were inducted into the Canadian Basketball Hall of Fame and the Victoria Sports Hall of Fame. They have been called the "peerless pair," the "Royal Couple of Roundball" and "Mr. and Mrs. Basketball." They also made history by becoming the first husband and wife to coach national teams simultaneously in Canada. However, their careers have not been without the odd bad pass or fumble. When Canada's team finished seventh in the 1994 world championships, Ken faced intense media criticism. He was also accused of racism when he cut two black men from the team. He vehemently denied it, and an inquiry declared that the charges were unfounded. He decided to leave the national team in 1995 and become the president of the federal-provincial Commonwealth Centre for Sport Development, an organization with the goal to develop Canada's athletes and coaches. He spent four years there before becoming the coach of a professional team in Tokyo. More recently, health issues became a problem for Kathy, and eventually required that she officially step down as head coach in March of 2005.

Now, the Shields' are spending more time at their home at 10 Mile Point and less time travelling the world to coach teams, recruit players and attend clinics. Their television is no longer a non-stop display of basketball. The Shields' devotion to basketball often meant spending months apart and going without holidays. The "Royal Couple of Roundball" have earned their crowns.

The Dairy Farmers Who Preserved Saanich's Open Spaces

THE ROGERS FAMILY

Mr and Mrs George Rogers with daughter Beatrice (Saanich Archives 1978-3-15)

Lillie Rogers: – 1925
George Rogers: – 1943

Before the Victoria and Sidney Railway closed in 1919, a wood-burning train dubbed the Cordwood Limited ran from Victoria through the Saanich Peninsula. One of the stops along the way was at Rogers Crossing at Chester Lea farm. When the Rogers' pond on Christmas Hill froze in the winter, the train would deposit a cargo of eager skaters to the makeshift rink and pick them up hours later, after their noses and ears had turned red with cold and the sun had disappeared from the sky.

Christmas Hill has housed some of Saanich's most diligent citizens and pioneers: Bruce Hutchison, the Bridgmans and the Rogers. These families all resisted the development pressures encroaching on their properties and delayed selling until the situation became impossible. In fact, the Rogers' family was one of the last working family farms in Saanich, and as a result, Christmas Hill is one of the largest remaining open spaces within the urban core of Greater Victoria.

George Rogers Sr. left his father's mill in Cheshire, England, in 1885. He worked in a Toronto hat factory for a year before he travelled west (on one of the first trains to cross Canada) and arrived on Vancouver Island. He worked at the Medina Farm in James Bay for a year before becoming a tenant farmer at Craigie Lea Farm. He bought a dairy herd and married Lillie Stevens in 1887.

In 1898, the Rogers purchased the 225 acre Alderley Farm on Agnes Road. George dropped the name "Alderley" when another Saanich resident claimed that he had priority to the name, and rather than make a fuss, the Rogers' farm became the Chester Lea Farm.

Later he sold part of the Chester Lea farm and bought land at 821 Rogers Avenue. In 1925, Lillie died, and George built a second farmhouse at 931 Woodhall Drive for himself and his daughters. George's son, George Jr., continued to supply milk under the Chester Lea Diary name from 1920 – 1958. In 1930, George Jr. married Genevieve. For 38 years, George Jr. personally attended to the milk run every day.

By 1958 the 255-acre farm had dwindled to about 50 acres. One of George and Genevieve's daughters, Phyllis, married Richard Fatt, and they ran a poultry farm behind their house on Dieppe Road on the last parcel of land. The Fatt family ran it for three generations until encroaching suburbia and neighbours complaining of the smell persuaded them to sell the farm.

The efforts of the Hutchison, Bridgman and Rogers families to preserve the rural character of Christmas Hill weren't entirely fruitless: on The Rogers' side of the hill, sixty-eight hectares of Garry oak meadows were purchased by the Land Conservancy of British Columbia and included

The Rogers Family swimming at Cordova Bay, c1918
(Saanich Archives 1978-3-8)

in the Christmas Hill Nature Sanctuary. Garry oak meadows are one of the most threatened ecosystems in the country; in Canada they can only be found on southern Vancouver Island and in some areas of the Fraser Valley.

There are several roads in Saanich named after members of the Rogers family: Lily Avenue, after George Sr.'s wife; Genevieve Road, after George Jr.'s wife; Chesterlea Road, after the farm; and Rogers Avenue was named to commemorate the entire family.

Reviving Saanich History

DAVID LAI

Dr. David Chuenyan Lai

When the Ross Bay Cemetery opened in 1873, a section on the water's edge was designated for "Aborigines and Mongolians." The first Chinese man buried was interred as "Chinaman #1," the second as "Chinaman #2," and so on. But for many, the cemetery was not a final resting place; storms routinely flooded the area and washed the coffins out to sea.

Attempting to find a more permanent burial ground, the Chinese Consolidated Benevolent Association bought approximately eight acres near Swan Lake. But the first time a funeral procession made their way to the lot, they were turned away by an angry mob of white farmers. The Chinese had to sell the land they had legally bought and paid for, and instead purchased 3.5 acres on Harling Point, but encountered the same problem: the first funeral procession was interrupted by another mob. Fortunately, this time a policeman was present. He arrested the man with the smoking shotgun, and the Chinese could continue.

Few people know the history behind the Chinese cemetery at Harling Point in Oak Bay, and even fewer people know about the attempts to create a cemetery near Swan Lake. But thanks to Dr. David Lai, who dedicated much of his career to preserving the knowledge of Chinese heritage buildings, sites and history, the stories of

(Courtesy UVic Archives 0081300211)

the Chinese in Victoria are more accessible than ever before.

Victoria's Chinatown is the only one in North America that has original 19th century buildings, and his efforts at preserving the area and writing the book, *The Forbidden City Within Victoria: Myth, Symbol and Streetscape of Canada's Earliest Chinatown* were recognized when he became a Member of the Order of Canada and received the Gabrielle Leger award (Heritage Canada's most prestigious award).

He has also made significant contributions to the Saanich community and has been involved in numerous projects, including a program designed to strengthen children's awareness of heritage. He served as a member of the Saanich Heritage Advisory and Archival Committee, and his work in establishing criteria and methodology for residential building restoration in Saanich won him a Heritage Society of B.C award in 1985.

But all of his awards and success preserving Victoria's Chinese history might never have happened if he'd been a better liar. Lai, who was born in Hong Kong, earned a PhD from the London School of Economics and fully intended to go back to a teaching position in Hong Kong after a brief time as a visiting lecturer at UVic. He received a written invitation from the government to immigrate, and when he revealed that to the University of Hong Kong, his teaching job dissolved, and Lai was left scrambling to find a job in Canada.

So he began his career at UVic as an assistant professor in the geography department in 1968, and examples of his work can be found all over Victoria. The Chinese herbalist shop in the Chinatown exhibit in the Royal B.C. Museum was secured thanks to his influence; his research also lead to Harling Point and Chinatown being designated as national historic districts or sites.

He was instrumental in establishing 13 scholarships and awards for students: five undergraduate, five graduate and three travel awards to China or Chinatowns outside Victoria.

After thirty years of researching and writing about Canada's Chinese Community, Lai retired as a full professor with two teaching awards, and planned to keep the promise to his wife that he would learn to cook.

The Compassionate Judge
WILLIAM OSTLER

Judge William Ostler: 1915 – 2003

"On his appointment, he brought a sense of dignity and decorum to his Court. He was unfailingly courteous to those who appeared before him and he earned the respect and admiration of everyone. The guilty, who should have known better, were eloquently chided for their misdemeanours or sternly rebuked for more heinous offences. However, those unfortunate individuals, who had been caught up in the criminal justice system by reason of tragic personal or family circumstances or who were disadvantaged because of their ethnic or racial background, were often the beneficiaries of his compassion and wisdom."

(Courtesy Victoria Law Courts)

When Judge William Leonard Ostler was presented with an honorary doctor of laws degree from the University of Victoria in 1986, the senate's speech stated that he was one of British Columbia's most respected authorities on criminal law and procedure – though Judge Ostler had never been to law school, and his sole knowledge of court procedure arose from his time as a clerk in the courthouse. When he officially retired in 1981, he was the last lay judge in B.C.

While Judge Ostler received some criticism for his background, it was generally acknowledged that he had an "encyclopaedic knowledge" of the law. He presided in Victoria for over 25 years, first as Magistrate, then as Judge, and finally as Administrative Judge of the Provincial Court.

He was born on December 6, 1915, and attended Cedar

Hill Elementary School and Victoria High School. After graduating, he worked as a clerk at the Fisgard Street courthouse in Victoria. His only extended period away from Saanich was when he served as a naval officer in the North Atlantic during the Second World War (he retired a lieutenant-commander.) After the war, he returned to Saanich and would live in the area with his wife Kathleen until he died in 2003.

When he started work as a clerk, he began to keep a scrapbook of newspaper articles about any particularly humorous, scandalous or horrific cases. The articles reveal that in the 1940's, lashes were still meted out as punishment, "vagrancy" was punishable by jail time, and the results of police shooting competitions were considered prime news.

Throughout his career, Judge Ostler had close ties to the police department. In addition to being the police court clerk, he was also a member of the fingerprint bureau. In 1936, he attended his first shooting competition after only a year of practise, (called the Domino Chief Constables' Shoot) and outdid many of the department's leading marksmen. He tied for the leading score of 49 out of 50, even though they had to load the gun for him, because he'd never shot an automatic before. He won two medals.

In 1947, he was nominated for the position of deputy chief of the Victoria Police Department. Though he had strong support from the police chief and the mayor, one commissioner felt that he was too valuable as a clerk, and was concerned that he had no previous police experience. So he asked to have his name withdrawn from consideration. He wouldn't accept the position unless it was with unanimous approval.

If Judge Ostler were criticized, it was usually for being slightly lenient to the accused. He was more likely to grant bail, and offered people more time to pay fines, than many other judges on the bench at that time.

While he often expressed sympathy towards people in his court, he was extremely strict with drug traffickers, and in one case said, "The crime of heroin trafficking is assassination by instalments. It is a crime of indescribable wickedness". When Ottawa gave judges the option to give first-time drug offenders an absolute or conditional discharge, he firmly rejected the idea.

Judge Ostler retired in December of 1981, but served as the Director of the Legal Services Society of B.C. for many years. An avid gardener, he was a founding member of the Friends of the University of Victoria Gardens group, and helped plan, maintain and improve the gardens that held a rare collection of rhododendrons.

Though he didn't have the conventional education that judges rely on today, he brought compassion, understanding and an unparalleled knowledge of the law to the bench – making him one of the best practitioners of law in the history of British Columbia.

Forty Years of Community Service
RUSS MORGAN

Russ Morgan

When Reserve Staff Sergeant Russ Morgan turned in his uniform in 2002, it marked the end of 40 years of dedicated volunteer service with the Saanich Police Department. Though Russ had no shortage of demands on his time - including co-owning and operating a successful business and raising a family – he rarely missed his Thursday night shift, and it is estimated that he was the longest serving volunteer police officer in Canada.

There are currently 28 volunteer members of the Saanich Police Department Reserve Program. In Russ Morgan's day, reserve constables assisted in road blocks, public relations, patrol work and crime prevention; they were also there to offer support when the work load overwhelms the regular police officers. Sometimes they were also involved in more hands-on police work, as in the time when Russ and a partner were on regular patrol and noticed the front door of a store had been kicked in. When they stopped to investigate, they discovered two people stealing cigarettes.

(Courtesy Saanich Police Department)

When they were spotted, the two suspects ran, and Russ caught one and his partner arrested the other one.

Russ began his police career as a civil defence auxiliary constable in 1961, when the Saanich police department was still located in Royal Oak. His shift usually started at 7:00 p.m., and if it was quiet, he would go home around midnight. If it was a busy night, he would stay later. It might be searching for a lost child, pursuing a suspect who was running away from the scene of the crime, or guarding captured suspects. The next morning, he would be back working at his day job.

When Russ first began to volunteer, he thought he would like to become a regular police officer. Then he thought about working the night shift. However, as a reserve officer, he got to do many of the same things a regular officer did, without the paperwork. He decided to keep his volunteer position, and took over his father's role as co-owner and manager of Stockers Moving and Storage.

As the senior reserve officer in Saanich, Russ saw hundreds of both reserve and regular members go through the system. He became the link between the reserves and the regular force, and many people relied on him for advice and counsel. Russ was a respected member of the department; many reserve officers went on to become regular police members, and often the recruiting officers would ask Russ's opinion of the candidate before hiring them. Many regular officers have stories of how Russ "saved their bacon" when they were new to the job. Many times he was in as much danger as the regular members, but as a reserve, he was seldom allowed to carry a gun.

Russ was frequently involved with training simulations for the reserve program. Whether he was assisting in simulations of assaults, thefts or dealing with someone who was intoxicated, Russ was always a convincing actor. He was also a volunteer for local fundraising campaigns, community events and other police-related programs. He recruited other reserve members to collect money for the Multiple Sclerosis fundraising campaign, and would often help direct traffic at the Strawberry Festival or the Victoria Day Parade. He also worked on the Home Security Assessment Program and many other tasks to assist the police department.

Police work seems to run in the Morgan family. Russ's twin brother Ron was a Sergeant in Oak Bay, and his son Steve is a constable with the Saanich Police. His son-in-law Paul currently serves with the Central Saanich Police Department.

Russ won the C-FAX "Community Leader" award in 1999, and was also presented with the Queen's Golden Jubilee Medal. When Russ retired, many regular and reserve members, retired members and friends attended a dinner to honour the man who served under six police chiefs, influenced countless numbers of people, and devoted approximately 20,000 hours of his time to serving the community.

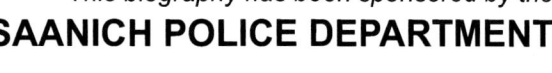

This biography has been sponsored by the
SAANICH POLICE DEPARTMENT

Mr. B.C. Tennis

GORDON HARTLEY

Gordon Francis Hartley: 1918 - 2004

For most tennis players, having a "long reach" usually refers to their skill at the game. But Gordon Hartley's long reach extended to a community. During his 50 years as a tennis coach, high school teacher and long distance runner on Vancouver Island, Hartley crossed - and influenced - the paths of hundreds of people.

Hartley's teaching career extended from 1939 to 1990, and was interrupted only by a four-year term serving as an Artillery Officer during the Second World War. Shortly after he returned from Western Europe, he graduated from the University of British Columbia and began teaching at Victoria High School, where he remained for 20 years.

In 1945, Victoria, Saanich and Esquimalt jointly sponsored the Greater Victoria public parks summer instructional program. The program began as an offshoot of the summer playground program (of which Hartley was director from 1945 to 1956) and offered three one-hour lessons per week to 20 children. Hartley taught children in the summer and adults in the spring and fall, and over the years, the program expanded to morning and evening lessons seven days a week from April through October. In the 1960's, more than 600 youth competed in Victoria's annual junior tournament. Several players went on to compete nationally.

An avid long distance runner, Hartley also coached the cross-country team. In 1954, he officiated at the Vancouver British Empire Games and served as the Track Judge at the finish line for the legendary Bannister-Landry "Miracle Mile."

Roger Bannister had been the first to break the four-minute mile in 1954, but seven weeks later, John Landry performed the same feat. Hartley was chosen to officiate in a race between the two record-breakers, and so he had a perfect view to see history made as Bannister beat Landry to the finish line.

In 1971, Hartley became an English Instructor and Dean of Students at Camosun College. He retired from full-time teaching in 1978, but continued to teach English in the Continuing Studies department until 1990.

If there is a gene for tennis, it seems to run in the Hartley family: Gordon's son Russ is the Head Tennis Professional at the Vancouver Lawn Tennis and Badminton Club, and Russ's son Sean has also become an instructor there.

In addition to his teaching and coaching responsibilities, Hartley furthered interest and knowledge by writing articles about the Victoria tennis scene for the Islander section of the Times Colonist newspaper. He praised the sport for becoming a more affordable and long-lasting pastime.

In recognition of decades of work as a player and a coach, the British Columbia Tennis Association named him "Mr. B.C. Tennis" in 1979, and the Cedar Hill indoor tennis facility was named after him in 1994.

Hartley believed that tennis was more than a game; he considered the sport a social equalizer. In an Islander article, he wrote, "it [tennis] is a great leveller, one of the ultimate democratizers, for one leaves all the hard-earned accomplishments of the rest of his life behind him when he steps on the court. Your doctorate in physics does you no good in returning a fast twist serve; being president of your own company does you no good in putting topspin on a backhand drive.

"Tennis forces us to put aside all the carefully contrived disguises, defences and social stratagems we've spent so much time building, and start all over. Truly a conflict between expectations and reality. As any tennis player will confirm, this has to be the principal reason we keep playing the game".

Camosun College (Courtesy Barry F. King)

Commonwealth Place Pool (Courtesy Saanich Parks and Recreation)

Lochside Trail (Courtesy Saanich Planning Department)

1986 - 1995

Many remember the Roads and Parks and Recreation Referendums of 1989 when Saanich approved $10 million to be invested in community recreation centres and another $5 million for parks acquisition and development. Outdoor recreation sites, such as Tyndall and McMinn parks opened, Beckwith Park added a new playground area with basketball and tennis courts, and in 1995, the Galloping Goose bicycle and walking trail was completed. Saanich hosted the B.C. Festival of the Arts in 1989 and constructed Saanich Commonwealth Place in order to help host the Commonwealth Games in 1994. Thousands of volunteers donated their time and energy towards making the international event a success. Saanich continued its international involvement in 1988 with the initiation of its involvement with the municipality of Zomba, Malawi, in Southern Africa through a program funded by the Canadian International Development Agency.

In the midst of park and recreation centre additions, the construction of new housing and shopping complexes continued throughout these years. Townhouses were built in Gordon Head, Broadmead and Cadboro Bay, a four-theatre cinema was constructed at University Heights mall, and shopping centres emerged at Ravine Way and Blanshard, and in Broadmead. After severe damage caused by a fire in 1989, the Nellie McClung Library reopened its doors in 1991, and three years later the Bruce Hutchison Library opened. A 1992 agreement with the Coast Salish people for use of the Gorge Waters and Saanich Park property ensured the continued enjoyment of parks for all residents in the area.

The Music Man

DAVID FOSTER

(Courtesy Matthew Rolston)

David Foster: 1950 -

at work, where he was the superintendent at the Saanich Municipal Yard. A piano and organ player himself, Maurie was so excited that he rushed to his Saanich home to watch his son, and didn't go back to work that afternoon. Six months later, David won an award at the Victoria Music Festival.

Music was a large part of the Foster family. David and his six sisters went to piano lessons once a week, which at that time were fifty cents each, and Maurie played the organ at St. Luke's and Elk Lake Churches on Sundays. When he was 13, David received a summer music scholarship to Washington. He returned home to go to high school at Mount Douglas High School, but left in grade 11 to travel with Chuck Berry's backup band to England, effectively launching his professional music career. He stayed in England for a year, came home when he was 17 and finished grade 12.

Eleanor Foster was dusting the piano, producing a random cacophony of notes and chords, when her five-year-old son David began naming the notes she was hitting. He was so accurate that Eleanor phoned her husband Maurie

David Foster's first big hit was "Wildflower" with the band Skylark – words by Saanich Police Officer Dave Richardson. He became a sought-after session musician and pianist, appearing with stars like John Lennon and Rod Stewart. His production career began in 1976, and in 1979, he won his first Grammy award for penning "After the Love Has Gone" by Earth, Wind and Fire. From there, his career flourished, and he became one of pop music's most successful producers.

To date, David has won 14 Grammys and an unprecedented 42 nominations for the album, record and producer of the year awards. He has also received three Academy Award nominations, two Gemini Awards and five Juno Awards. He was inducted into the Canadian Music Hall of Fame in 1998, was made an officer of the Order of Canada in 2004 and an officer to the Order of British Columbia in 1995. The University of Boston and the University of Victoria have awarded him doctorates in music. His music has appeared in movies like *Moulin Rouge, The Bodyguard, Quest for Camelot* and many others. His protégées are everywhere, and among the successful artists he's worked with are Celine Dion, Barbra Streisand Paul McCartney and Madonna. In 1971 David moved to Los Angeles, where he currently resides.

David is also well known through British Columbia for his philanthropic work. In 1986, he established the David Foster Foundation, a charity to help children in British Columbia who require organ transplants. The Foundation covers many of the non-medical expenses of the procedure. This may include rent, mortgage payments, accommodations or child care for other siblings while the family is away. The Foundation has organized many fundraising events, from celebrity softball games (in which Wayne Gretsky once played with a hockey stick) to charity galas.

David is also the volunteer music director for the Andre Agassi Foundation, which has raised over $7 million for underprivileged children, and the Mohamed Ali Foundation, which has raised over $3 million for Parkinson's disease. Foster also co-wrote and recorded *Tears Are Not Enough*, a fundraiser for famine victims in Africa. Proceeds from the CD, which featured musicians like Bryan Adams, Joni Mitchell and Neil Young, had raised over $3.2 million by 1990.

In 2004, Foster was promoted from a member to an officer in the Order of Canada, in recognition of his philanthropy and lifetime achievement.

The Heir to Pavarotti

RICHARD MARGISON

Richard Margison: 1953 –

Richard Margison is a lirico spinto, a tenor who can infuse drama and power into the grand Italiante climaxes. He has performed in the world's top opera houses, including the Sydney Opera, the Vienna Staatsoper and the Metropolitan Opera. But he wasn't always an opera devotee. In the 70's, he sang light rock and folk music in Victoria bars and coffeehouses. After a year of general studies at the University of Victoria, he applied to become a performance major in the music program – and was turned down, because the panel said he had "no promise."

Richard was adopted into a musical family (a request by his birth mother) when he was a week old. His father was a violinist for the Victoria Symphony, and his mother was a piano teacher. He completed his education in the Saanich public school system before enrolling at UVic.

Fortunately, his failed application to UVic didn't deter him from music; in fact, he dug his

(Courtesy Victoria Conservatory of Music)

heels in and became more determined to make music a career. Selena James, a voice coach at the Victoria Conservatory of Music, was on the panel, and she believed that he had great potential. She cited his broad chest, tongue control and excellent coloratura. She became his teacher, and she was right – Richard is now one of the most recognized tenors in the world, and some critics and professionals call him the heir to the legendary Luciano Pavarotti.

He started his career performing for companies like the Bastion Theatre, local Gilbert and Sullivan shows and the Canada Opera Piccola. In 1980, he made his Pacific Opera Victoria debut with the production, *The Barber of Seville*. His big break came in 1988, when he successfully auditioned for the English National Opera. A few years later, he was performing for larger companies, and by 1990, he had his first performance in Europe. After his successful performances of Verdi's *Ballo in Maschera*, he never had to audition again.

In addition to having a "giant tenor voice," Richard is known for exhibiting a style and finesse that, while unorthodox, can bring a humorous flair to the often-solemn world of opera. He is considered a specialist in Verdi and Puccini, but he has always wanted to play the Cowardly Lion in a production of the *Wizard of Oz*.

His permanent residence is now in Toronto with his wife, opera director and violist Valerie Kuinka, and their daughter, Lauren (a budding opera singer herself.) Valerie is the founder and director of "Collaborations: A Chamber Arts Experience," a multi-disciplinary performance series that combines performance and visual arts. Valerie directs several performances a year in the Toronto area. Singing 10 operas a year means Richard doesn't spend as much time with his family as he would like; he is often away for eight to nine months of the year. He plans to cut back on his touring career when he reaches age 60.

He often returns to his hometown to sing for fundraising events for the Victoria Conservatory of Music and the Pacific Opera. In 1994, he performed the song that marked the finale of the opening ceremony to the Commonwealth Games.

He was named an Officer of the Order of Canada and named an Honorary Citizen of Victoria, along with Atom Egoyan and Nelly Furtado, in 2001. He became the 44th member to be inducted into the Canadian Opera Hall of Fame in 2003. And, in an ironic twist, perhaps to make up for that long-ago verdict that stated he had no promise, Richard received an honorary doctorate in music from UVic in 1996.

An Extraordinary Achiever

ROY VICKERS

(Courtesy Times Colonist)

Roy Henry Vickers: 1946 –

When Roy Henry Vickers attempted to join the RCMP, he discovered that he had a form of colour blindness that makes it difficult to discern gradations in colour. When the RCMP learned of his condition, they refused his application.

Fortunately, the Saanich Fire Department didn't consider his eye condition a problem, and promptly hired him. Even more fortunately, the hundreds of people who are fans of his artwork don't seem to think it's a problem either, and over the years, Vickers has built a successful career and gained an international reputation as an artist. His work has been presented to Queen Elizabeth II, former U.S. president Bill Clinton and former Soviet President Boris Yeltsin, among others. In 1998, he was inducted into the Order of British Columbia, and in 1994, Maclean's Magazine named him one of Canada's "extraordinary achievers."

Vickers was the head designer of the Saanich Commonwealth Place recreation facility that was built for the 1994 Commonwealth Games, and the structure was certainly an extraordinary achievement that made him well deserving of recognition. The building, with three totem poles placed at the main entrance, is designed using the concept of a longhouse. A nine-panel frieze decorates the front of the building; it depicts elders and chiefs from each of the five Pacific Northwest nations. Inside, Vickers created two murals on the pool wall that represent the legend of a brother and sister who bring the salmon back to B.C. every year.

Vickers was born in Greenville, in Northern B.C. His father was a native fisherman and his mother was a nurse who was adopted into the Tsimshian tribe before Roy was born. Vickers' parents and five siblings came to Saanich when he was 17. Roy's sister Margaret became well known in the community when she was voted "Queen of Saanich" in 1966, during the municipality's 60th Jubilee. Not long after Vickers became a Saanich firefighter, he left to attend the Gitanmaax School of Northwest Indian Art at 'Ksan on the Skeena River.

While Vickers received the Maclean's magazine award for his work on Commonwealth Place, he was also recognized for his involvement with Vision Quest, a fund to establish a recovery and treatment centre in British Columbia. Vickers had spent time in an Arizona treatment facility for drug and alcohol addiction, and he wanted to see similar services available on Vancouver Island.

In partnership with the RCMP, Vickers organized several fundraisers for Vision Quest, including art on Roger's Chocolate boxes and a CD that featured Roch Voisine, Dan Hill and other artists. He also organized a canoe voyage from Hazelton to Victoria, and a concert at Royal Roads University that featured Raffi, Prairie Oyster and Murray McLauchlan.

Vickers continues to be involved with various fundraising campaigns in the community. He lost an aunt, two friends and his mother to cancer, and so in 2003, he raised $32,000 for the Cops for Cancer fundraising campaign by donating the proceeds from the sale of a limited edition print, Sandcastles.

Vickers currently owns two galleries. The most successful gallery, Eagle Aerie Gallery, is in Tofino and receives over 200,000 visitors a year. The Roy Henry Vickers Gallery, opened in 2004, is currently in Sidney.

Vickers's first coffee table book, *Solstice: The Art of Roy Vickers* was published in 1998 and became a bestseller. In 1996, a documentation of the carving of a 30-foot Salmon Pole of the 1994 Games became his second book: *A Spirit Transformed: A Journey from Tree to Totem.* In 2003, a second coffee table book entitled *Copperman: The Art of Roy Henry Vickers* was published.

In 1994, the Saanich Commonwealth Place served as a representative of Canada to other Commonwealth nations, and continues to be a facility in which people can compete and play. Vickers donated much of his time and energy to creating a design suitable for a world-class venue, and now citizens of Saanich and the surrounding communities can enjoy it for many years to come.

This biography has been sponsored by
Cordova Bay Community Association
Roger Stonebanks – President   (250) 658-5125

Special Places. Forever, for Everyone

BILL TURNER

(Courtesy The Land Conservancy of BC)

Bill Turner: 1944 -

"It gets in your blood and you can't stop—it becomes an addiction."

When Bill Turner said this in an interview in 2002, he wasn't talking about his past duties as a Saanich police officer, nor his role as a realtor dealing with exotic Caribbean resort properties. The addiction Bill can't get out of his system is a dedication to preserving the land in his own backyard. Unlike most realtors, Bill is not interested in land to develop or sell for a quick personal profit. Instead, his goal is to leave land as it is, or restore it to its original state for the benefit of the community.

Bill's first work in land preservation was with the Nature Conservancy of Canada in 1992, in his role as Tourism Victoria's representative on a committee working to purchase what is now Gowland Tod Provincial Park. When the project finally came together in 1994, Bill knew he was hooked, and would continue to work with the organization for several years. He soon realized that when working at a national level however, local areas in need can be overlooked. With this need in mind, Bill and four other founding members created The Land Conservancy of B.C. in 1997.

Local areas would seem to be a bit of an understatement. Before moving the TLC head office to Craigflower National Historic Site in 2002, Bill housed the administrative offices of TLC rent-free in the basement of his Old West-Saanich home, which he built on his days off from the police force. He started in the reserves, and stayed for 12 years, working his way up to youngest Corporal in the department's history. Though he misses the camaraderie of police work, Bill's eventual shift into real estate was determined by a desire to work independently. He seems to have found a good compromise in TLC, where the inventive land deals he works are for the benefit of many.

TLC's founders modeled the organization on the U.K.'s National Trust, with the long-term vision and mandate to "protect areas of ecological importance, as well as areas of historic, cultural, scientific, scenic or compatible recreational value." TLC's motto, "Special Places. Forever, for Everyone" was demonstrated by its first project, the purchase of South Winchelsea Island for $600,000. The island, located in the Georgia Strait, is well-known for its Garry oak ecosystem, and plays host to scientists who come to study both the Island's ecosystem and marine mammals. Since this initial venture, the organization has purchased or restored over 30,000 hectares of land, and currently is working on the Ours Forever campaign, the goal of which

is to raise a minimum of $30 million to purchase and protect land in the Victoria area.

Beyond his role with TLC, Bill finds time to act in a volunteer capacity with numerous organizations. He is a founding member of the Land Trust Alliance of B.C., a past chairperson of the South Okanagan Similkameen Conservation Program, and has served on the boards of the B.C. Grasslands Conservation Council, the Pacific Coast Joint Venture, the Canadian Intermountain Joint Venture, the East Kootenay Conservation Program, the Saanich Inlet Protection Society, Veins of Life Watershed Society, and the Citizens Association to Save the Environment. Though he stepped down from his position as President of TLC in 2004, he continues to act as its executive director, and in the fall of 2005, he chaired sessions at the International Conference of National Trusts in Washington, D.C.

Bill acts out of a desire to protect our region's heritage, and his efforts have won him distinctions at local and national levels over the past eight years. In 2002, he was named the CFAX Community Leader of the Year, as well as the City of Victoria's Citizen of the Year, and in August, 2005, he was named a member of the Order of Canada, the highest honour for lifetime achievement awarded in Canada. Though he seems to regard his efforts as a natural and everyday course of action, thanks to Bill, Saanich and Victoria residents will have protected land to enjoy in the future.

Corporal Bill Turner with Chief Peterson, 1974
(Saanich Archives 1984-6-32)

This biography has been sponsored by

Joan Outerbridge in "Shangri-la" (Courtesy Times Colonist)

A Paradise for Birds and Butterflies
JOAN OUTERBRIDGE

Joan Outerbridge

Clearly, Joan Outerbridge is a serious gardener. She settled at 1171 Royal Oak Drive in 1987, and has transformed the property from a bare, swampy marsh to a paradise of flowers, trees, birds and butterflies. She calls it *Shangri-la*, after the mythical land in Tibet where travellers found peace and tranquillity from the outside world. Joan's *Shangri-la* was designed for this purpose, but the travellers in her mind are of the feathered variety.

Visitors—human ones, that is—experience a sense of awe when approaching Joan's garden, especially when they learn that the majority of work was done in under five years. The entrance to the garden is a shaded pathway surrounded by forest and tall grasses that opens into a burst of colour from May through October. Inside *Shangri-la*, the hum of traffic and construction is replaced by birdsong.

The bird life is an important part of Joan's design for the garden. She has planted over 30 waring spruce to attract them, and hidden six feeding stations in tree branches throughout her 8.5 acre property. What distinguishes the garden from others is not just its size and beauty, but its design and careful plant selections, like buddleias, thyme and black-eyed susans, which attract birds and butterflies.

The decision to turn her garden into a bird sanctuary was made around midnight when Joan woke to the squawks of a mother duck who was being attacked in her nest. Joan decided to find a way to protect the ducks and birds that made their homes on her property. The tiny island she built for them would be her most ambitious project to date. The swampy pond first had to be excavated, then built up with rock to preserve the plant beds she envisioned around it. When she finished, spring visitors could stroll around the path, surrounded by rhododendrons, hoping to spot the new ducklings.

The duck pond is one in a network of small ponds and waterfalls that run through the property, curving around the leafy trees, alongside the Japanese-inspired rock garden and through a wildflower area filled with roses. She planted every cultivated flower and tree herself, working with the natural lay of the land. Not any gardener would tackle such projects as building ponds, waterfalls and islands, or plant with the birds and butterflies in mind, but Joan isn't any gardener. She attended the Pennsylvania School of Horticulture, and worked as a landscape architect in her home country, Bermuda. When she traded her tropical island for Vancouver Island, the excavators, truckloads of rock, and thousands of trees and plants followed soon after her arrival.

So how much upkeep did a garden like Joan's entail? The down-to-earth gardener admits that the majority of her day was spent working outdoors, but she wasn't complaining. In fact, she laughed when visitors suggested she lighten her work load by installing an underground sprinkler system. She prefered to water all the plants by hand, with 600 feet of hose that hang on 12 enormous wheels against her garage. She was even known to row out to her tiny island to make sure the plants were thriving.

Though the pond is an immediate focal point for visitors to *Shangri-la*, it is an 85 year old Golden Nectar plum tree that Joan claims, "makes the garden." She rescued the tree from a construction site near Shelbourne and North Dairy in 1988, moving it on a low-bed around 2 a.m. one night to avoid disrupting traffic. Her other rescue missions included a flowering plum from Sidney and an English yew from Esquimalt.

Joan's plan was to establish the garden as a perpetual trust, maintain the work she has done, and leave the rest to nature. In 2005, *Shangri-la* was purchased by Saanich Municipality as a nature and bird sanctuary.

The Soccer Star

IAN BRIDGE

(Courtesy Times Colonist)

Ian Bridge

Growing up in Saanich, Ian Bridge excelled at hockey, basketball and track, but it was soccer that turned out to be his favourite, and he played the sport at the highest level. As a youth he became the offensive star for Lakehill, but remained an all-round athlete, winning the Victoria High School's Outstanding Athlete award in 1977 and 1978. During his years at Victoria High School, Ian was a member of Canada's Junior team, playing in 16 international matches between 1976 and 1979. He won a Canada Games gold medal with the B.C. side, then moved to Britain where he trained with West Ham and played for Maidstone United. Ian spent his last season as an amateur with Seattle before turning professional in 1980. That season he helped the Sounders win the North American Soccer League (NASL) Trans Atlantic Cup.

Injury kept Ian on the sidelines for the 1980 World Cup, but he made up for it the following year with an impressive World Cup debut. He scored from a defensive position in his first two matches in the

1981 games. He was also a pivotal player on the Canadian Olympic team that reached the quarter-finals in Los Angeles in 1984, and played in all of Canada's final three games at the 1986 World Cup in Mexico. Ian finished his playing career on the back line with five seasons in the Swiss Pro League and in Canada with the Victoria Vistas, Kitchener Kickers and North York Rockets. In all, he played in 124 NASL matches over six seasons, and over 100 matches for Canada, 33 of which were full internationals.

After retiring his cleats as a player, Ian turned to coaching and led the successful Canadian Women's team to the final of the U-19 FIFA World Cup in 2002, where they lost a heart-breaker to the U.S. in "golden goal" time. Nevertheless, the silver medal is the greatest accomplishment by a Canadian team at a FIFA tournament. In 2003, he was among the class inducted into the Victoria Sports Hall of Fame for his contributions to Canadian soccer as both a player and a coach.

As coach of the Women's U-20 team, Ian traveled to Thailand in 2004 where Canada lost to China in the quarter-finals of the U-20 FIFA World Cup. The majority of the young team will play together at the 2006 World Cup hosted by Russia, and in 2007 when the international tournament will be hosted by Canada, with games in Victoria, Vancouver, Edmonton and Toronto.

To give back to the soccer community, Ian now conducts coaching clinics across Canada. He enjoys being around people who love the game, sharing his knowledge, experience and passion for the sport.

Follow Your Nose

ACE THE WONDER DOG

Ace "MacKenzie": 1991 – 2003

During his nine-year career, Saanich Police Constable Ace was responsible for 325 arrests. Though just a hair over 80 pounds, he was known to fearlessly tackle armed suspects, pursue them into lakes, through backyards and onto the roofs of buildings. In his efforts to fight crime, he once suffered a broken rib and heat stroke, but was always eager to get back to work.

Even after he was diagnosed with spinal myelopathy, a degeneration of the spinal cord, and autoimmune haemolytic anemia, a condition in which the body rejects and kills red blood cells, Ace was indefatigable. A provincial, national and world championship winner for his tracking abilities, Ace was also a stellar character, and was known for his loyalty, persistence and an excellent memory – with a fondness for belly rubs.

The tan and black German Shepherd was only 14 months old when he became a member of the Saanich Police Force. His partner, Sergeant Glen MacKenzie, had joined the RCMP in 1982 when he was 20. After four years with the RCMP in Alberta, MacKenzie and his wife, Shannon, moved to Saanich where MacKenzie joined the municipal police.

MacKenzie originally became involved with the canine unit as a volunteer perpetrator in police dog training, but in 1990, he asked his supervisor if he could be a "dog man." His request was granted, and MacKenzie began what would become a long process of selecting a dog. Six months and 16 days later, he finally found Ace through the New Westminster Police Service.

When Ace was sent on the search for a ball in a field of tall grass, he searched for 40 minutes before finally giving up – the average time for a dog with "potential" is seven or eight minutes. In another test, in which a perpetrator runs from the dog before turning and threatening the animal, Ace again proved better than the average when he stood his ground (in training, 99 per cent of dogs run away in this test.) In three months, Ace became a certified police dog, and on June 22, 1992, the new team was on duty.

Sergeant Glen MacKenzie with Ace
(Courtesy Saanich Police Department)

Three years later, MacKenzie noticed that Ace had begun to walk strangely. After weeks of testing, the vet diagnosed him with degenerative myelopathy, a disease that is not unlike multiple sclerosis. Usually, the progress of the disease starts in paralysis that moves up the spine until it eventually paralyzes the lungs. At the time, the vet said that Ace wouldn't likely be able to work for longer than another month or so and that in six months, his hind legs could become paralyzed.

Before the diagnosis, MacKenzie and Ace had been training for the Canadian Police Canine Association Trials in Vancouver. MacKenzie decided to take Ace despite his illness, believing that the dog would rather be working than left at home. Three months after the diagnosis, Ace and MacKenzie competed against 35 other teams to win the championship. When the local paper covered the dog's success, they also wrote that, tragically, it would be Ace's last competition.

But five year old Ace had other ideas. A month later, an experimental medication put the disease into remission, and Ace made a "miraculous" recovery. Within two months, he was happily back at work.

Then, in July of 1998, Ace suffered another health crisis when he was diagnosed with autoimmune haemolytic anemia, a rare condition in which the body rejects and kills the red blood cells necessary for carrying oxygen from the lungs. That night, he required a blood transfusion. Over the next two weeks, the weakened dog made a slow recovery, but MacKenzie enforced a two-month holiday. Finally, he took Ace tracking, and the dog performed like he'd never had a break. On September 4th, Ace won the Canadian Police Canine Association Trials for the third time, without a single training session.

Ace retired and enjoyed two years of being a house dog with the MacKenzie family before he died of natural causes on April 14, 2003. He was 12 years old.

During his nine-year career, Ace became something of a legend among police dogs. He was the top dog overall several times in the B.C. Police Canine Championships and the Canadian National Police Canine Championships; he was also the top dog in obedience and agility at the World Police Canine Championships. His story even made it into an edition of Readers Digest in 2000, and he and Glen MacKenzie were featured on the front cover.

Sgt. MacKenzie is now considered one of Canada's premier police canine trainers, and Ace will be remembered as the dog who overcame tremendous obstacles, followed his nose and made Saanich a safer community.

This biography has been sponsored by the
SAANICH POLICE DEPARTMENT

From the Soccer Net to the Internet

JEFF MALLETT

Jeff Mallet accepts UVic Business' Distinguished
Entrepreneur of the Year Award, 2004
(Courtesy University of Victoria)

Jeff Mallett

When Yahoo! was started by two Stanford University students, it was called "Jerry Yang's Guide to the WWW," and was meant to be a simple search engine for use by other students. Its founders, Jerry Yang and David Filo, never thought it would become a wildly profitable business, and one of the world's most highly trafficked websites.

Mallett got his start in the Silicon Valley when he helped his professor at San Francisco State University (he was pursuing an MBA at the time, although he never completed it) to commercialize a business plan for a grammar and spellcheck software program. The company, called Reference Software, was sold to WordPerfect

in 1992; Mallett also founded WordPerfect's consumer division a year later.

When Jeff Mallett became Yahoo!'s 12th employee in 1995, the company was struggling. But the former Mt. Doug and UVic soccer star was instrumental in creating the business plan that turned the small search engine into a top global company, with a peak worth of $142 billion in share value. As Yahoo!'s president, Mallett oversaw over 4,000 employees in 25 countries.

He was also the general manager of Novell's worldwide consumer division, where he was responsible for product development and marketing communications. Then, when he was a 30 year old rising executive, a venture capitalist put him in touch with Yahoo! cofounders Jerry Yang, David Filo, and chief executive Tim Koogle. Though joining the fledgling company was risky, Mallett gambled – and won.

But it all could have been different, if Mallett had pursued a promising soccer career. Born in West Vancouver, his family moved to Vancouver Island when he was nine years old. He went to high school at Mt. Doug, and after he helped lead its soccer team to the 1982 B.C. high school title, he won a soccer scholarship to UVic. The team made it to the Canadian University Championship game, which they ultimately lost to McGill. He turned down a chance to go pro with the North American Soccer League (now defunct), and briefly was a member of both the Canadian National and Olympic teams.

Mallett's parents, Brian and Marilyn Mallett, gave Jeff his start in business when Brian left his secure job at B.C. Tel to open the Blethering Place

Tea Room in Oak Bay. Then, he established Island Pacific Telephone, one of the first interconnect companies that sold telephone hardware; Mallett began working for this company when he was a teenager. When he was an 18-year-old high school student, Mallett also got his general insurance license and worked on Saturdays for local insurance agent Ron Simpson.

In 2000, the National Post listed Mallett as one of the 50 richest Canadians, with a net worth of about $500 million (U.S.). That same year, he was 16th on Fortune magazine's list of "40 richest under 40."

In 2002, Mallett ended seven years at Yahoo! to spend more time with his wife Claire, and their daughters, Victoria and Amber. He renewed his commitment to sports, and became part owner of a major league baseball team, the San Francisco Giants (Mallett was a little leaguer as well as a soccer player.) He also became one of the main benefactors for the Victoria-based Canadian Baseball League.

In 2004, Mallet won the first "Distinguished Entrepreneur of the Year Award" from UVic's faculty of business; the award is intended to honour people who have had a significant and positive impact on the global community. He continues to be a participant and supporter of many charities, including the David Foster Foundation and the Boys and Girls Clubs of America.

Jeff Mallett's extraordinary success on the soccer field and in the dot-com world is a testament to his hard work and innovation – and to the very fortunate ability to see the difference between a risk, and an opportunity.

The Author who asked "Why?"

DIANE SWANSON

(Courtesy Diane Swanson)

Diane Swanson

Whether she is researching cockroaches or seals, rats or orangutans, Diane Swanson will root out quirky, surprising facts, and present them in a lively, appealing way. Swanson's passion for nature and attention to detail has made her one of North America's leading non-fiction children's authors, in part because she is so adept at answering her audience's perpetual question: "Why?"

Since her first nature book was published in 1992, Swanson has written 65 books, including the highly successful *Why Seals Blow their Noses* and *Animals Eat the Weirdest Things*. Much of her writing is aimed at children aged six to 12, although she has also written for preschoolers, teenagers and adults, and any one of her books contains information that can be appreciated by all ages. Her topics are always well researched, so even if you're not a fan of lice, you will certainly learn something about them that you didn't know before (for instance, did you know that scientists have discovered mummified lice on wooden combs belonging to ancient Egyptians?)

Growing up in Lethbridge, Alberta, Swanson liked to write, but didn't think writing was a feasible career. She was 18 when she sold her first story to a local newspaper, and she describes the event as a pivotal moment – she realized that she could sell her writing.

Swanson attended the University of Alberta, where she met her husband Wayne, who had also grown up in Lethbridge. After she graduated with a degree in Social Sciences, she volunteered to be a teacher for CUSO (Canadian University Service Overseas.) She didn't have a teaching degree, but there was such a great demand for teachers that they gave her a crash course before they sent her to the West Indies to teach English. There weren't many books at the school, so the students had to write in order to read, and Swanson had her first encounter with children and literature.

When Swanson came back from the West Indies, she took a job with the federal government in Ottawa. In 1974, she moved to Saanich and has lived there ever since. When she had her first child (she has a son, a daughter and two grandchildren), she began to freelance for

children's magazines, writing while her children napped or played. She also worked on a social studies textbook, published in 1985, and co-authored a book intended to teach children about racism. In the meantime, she approached several children's book publishers with proposals.

Then, Whitecap Books in North Vancouver approached Swanson with a book idea. Though Whitecap hadn't published children's books before, they did publish nature books, and it turned out that her first book was right in her backyard, or, more specifically, in the many creatures that live there. The book, called *A Toothy Tongue and One Long Foot*, was published in 1992, and since then she has never lacked for a book to write. She has won several awards, including the White Raven Selection of the International Youth Library, Munich, the American Orbis Pictus Award for Outstanding Non-fiction for Children, and the B.C. 2000 Book Award. She has won or been short-listed for many others.

Swanson plans to continue writing for children, because she finds that the curiosity and open-mindedness of most children allow her the freedom to write about subjects – such as rats and cockroaches – that most adults would be more interested in exterminating. When she isn't writing, Swanson travels to schools and public libraries to speak with children, though unlike many authors, she doesn't often read aloud from her work. She focuses on producing interactive presentations that get kids involved with the information and materials – the same philosophy that has made her books so popular for readers of many ages.

Saanich Caught the Spirit

THE COMMONWEALTH GAMES

1994 Commonwealth Games

The Victoria Commonwealth Games of 1994 was the largest celebration of sport and culture the city had ever seen. From August 18-28, 1994, more than 3,200 athletes from 66 Commonwealth nations gathered in the region to participate in an event second only to the Olympics in athletic competition. In addition to Olympic events, the Commonwealth Games also included sports that are played mainly in Commonwealth nations, such as lawn bowls and netball. At the '94 Games, the majority of events were held in Saanich at the University of Victoria's Centennial Stadium and the Commonwealth Pool, a $22 million structure in Royal Oak constructed specifically for the event. Mount Tolmie was the challenge for competitors in the Bicycle Road Races, which saw many streets in Saanich closed for this event.

Victoria, Saanich, and other municipalities in the regions set out to recruit 13,000 volunteers for the events. School students participated in the opening ceremonies, a 2,000-voice choir was compiled from local choral groups, and thousands of volunteers assisted with ceremonies, accreditation, transportation, sports and venue operations, administration and at the athletes village. Chairman of volunteer recruitment,

Chris Hall, was amazed by the overwhelming number of volunteers who devoted themselves to making the Games a success.

The Victoria Games boasted many firsts; 1994 was the first games where athletes with a disability competed as members of their national teams in aquatic, athletic, and lawn bowling events. This event was also the first time that arts and cultural events played such a large role in the celebrations. A year-long arts and cultural festival enhanced the Games, kicked off by the August 1, 1993 Symphony Splash at the Inner Harbour. For the following 12 months leading up to the games, people of all ages were given the chance to catch the spirit through the numerous dance, musical, film and cultural events that took place. As many as 28 groups and individuals showcased regional, national and international talent. In Saanich,

(Courtesy Saanich Parks & Recreation)

Saanich Commonwealth Place

gold medals and set two world records in a single race, breaking the 800 freestyle mark while setting a record time in the 1,500 freestyle.

By the end of the Games, many moments of glory, pride and mystery and shame had been recorded. For Canadians, we watched runners Angela Chalmers and Robyn Meagher take gold and silver in the 3,000 metres, Lisa Alexander take away two gold medals in synchronized swimming, and Casey Patton win the gold in flyweight boxing after three rounds. The Games also had its share of controversies. Athletes were stripped of medals due to drug use, while at least 10 athletes disappeared from the Games without explanation. Overall, however, visitors to Victoria and Saanich recalled the friendliness and organization of the volunteers and of the entire Games. The world watched South Africa compete in its first Commonwealth Games since the end of apartheid, and Hong Kong's last games before reverting from Britain to China in 1997.

the native participation committee hosted pow wows, traditional welcoming ceremonies, canoe races and a native theatre festival; the Victoria Youth Orchestra was in concert at the University of Victoria, which also organized a festival of Commonwealth films; Camosun College and the Art Gallery of Greater Victoria hosted a visual arts festival.

In the pool, Canada and Australia had the chance to rekindle the longtime rivalry between the two nations. Canada even brought back a favourite from the 1982 games in Brisbane: Captain Canada, the anonymous and highly patriotic swim team cheerleader dressed in a Canadian hockey jersey, black mask and Canadian flag cape. It would be the Aussies who ruled the pool in 1994 though. Keiren Perkins won four

It was agreed by all that in the year that Victoria welcomed the world, Saanich residents were treated to the greatest sports show we may ever see in this municipality.

Railways, Ethnobotany and History
NANCY & BOB TURNER

(Courtesy R. Turner)

Nancy Turner: 1947 –
Bob Turner: 1947 –

Did you know that that Victoria's beautiful native blue camas lilies were once a staple food of local First Nations, or that much of Saanich once was tended for camas production? Many other native plants of Saanich provide food, medicine and materials. Young stinging nettles are high in vitamin C and iron. Labrador tea, perhaps sweetened with licorice fern, makes a delicious beverage. And probably few people know that the combination of certain tree barks can help stomach pain, ulcers and kidney problems.

Ethnobotanist Nancy Turner knows all about the uses, benefits and healing properties of native plants. While the strict definition of ethnobotany is the study of the interrelationships between people and plants, Nancy has taken it a step farther and also researches the ethical issues around the knowledge and cultural uses of plants around the world.

Nancy's 35 years of working closely with First

Nations elders, who she always acknowledges as her teachers, to document their knowledge of plants and traditional ecological knowledge has earned her international recognition, and she is considered one of Canada's foremost ethnobotanists. She has won several prestigious awards, including the Lawson medal and the UVic Legacy Award, among others. She was made a Fellow of the Royal Society of Canada, was recognized as a Woman of Distinction in 1997 and Academic of the Year in 2002, was appointed to the Order of British Columbia in 1999, and has been honoured by the International Slow Food Organization. Over the course of her career, she has produced more than 150 publications, including at least 19 books.

Nancy has been interested in botany since she was four or five years old. She was born in California, but when her entomologist father, John Chapman and her mother Jane, moved with the family to Saanich, they settled on Ardersier Road, which is near Boleskine. More importantly, it is also within five miles of Francis Park, a spot she visited frequently. She joined the Victoria Junior Natural History Society, and trailed legendary naturalist Freeman King around meadows, marshes and up mountains.

Nancy met her future husband, Bob Turner, at Mount View high school. She enrolled in UVic and majored in botany; Bob pursued a degree in geography. After they completed their undergraduate degrees, Bob won a scholarship to UBC and graduated with an MSc in Regional Planning. Nancy skipped her MA and went directly to a PhD in botany and ethnobotany, writing her thesis on the plant taxonomic systems and ethnobotany of the First Nations of the Queen Charlottes, Bella Coola, and Lillooet regions.

The Turners married in 1969, and in 1973 they returned to Victoria. In 1975, the first of their three daughters was born. Over the next 15 years, Nancy wrote research papers and books but much of her time was involved in raising her children. It was by chance that she stumbled across an advertisement for a sessional teaching position at UVic, but it was skill and hard work that lead to her becoming a tenured distinguished professor in the School of Environmental Studies.

Nancy's husband, Bob, who was born in Victoria, is a noted historian and curator emeritus at the Royal British Columbia Museum. In 1974 he began working at the provincial museum to prepare exhibits for the Museum Train, and later became chief of historical collections.

Considered a leading authority on historical forms of transportation, Bob has written 14 books and numerous articles on railway and steamship history. He has won the Award of Merit of the American Association for State and Local History for the "continuing excellence" of his books, and three of his books have won the Canadian Railroad Historical Association's Book Award.

Camas bulbs and stinging nettles probably won't become commonplace on pantry shelves, but hopefully they will be part of the treasured landscape of Saanich, and Nancy's years of research will preserve the information and help perpetuate the traditional knowledge, wisdom and customs of First Nations people that have been threatened by cultural and environmental changes.

This biography has been sponsored by

Paul Bishop

A Gallery With a View

MAARTEN SCHADDELEE

(Courtesy Times Colonist)

Maarten Schaddelee: 1947 –

Nadine Schaddelee: 1947 –

You can tell that Maarten and Nadine Schaddelee's Gordon Head home is a little different as soon as you pull into the driveway. Sculptures of seals, eagles and whales stand near fountains; large slabs of coloured marble rest in a pile. The sculptures that are displayed on the lawn behind the house stand against a backdrop of the sky and ocean, where, if your timing is right, you might see a pod of orcas or a bald eagle.

This house-cum-art gallery, called Maarnada Studios, is the result of many years of hard work and careful thought on the part of Maarten and Nadine Schaddelee. While Maarten's art was displayed in galleries in the early years of his career, the Schaddelees wanted people who were interested in his work to have a richer experience. So they turned their home into a by-appointment gallery, where visitors are able to see the source of the inspiration for themselves.

Maarten has achieved world recognition for his sculptures of eagles, whales, dolphins and seals. He works in both marble and wood, and has branched out into sculptures representing mythological figures, such as Aquila, the bird of the Greek God Zeus. He says that he receives much of his inspiration from his property and its view – in fact, until he and Nadine moved into the house, he wasn't an artist. He worked in the family business, the Dutch Bakery on Fort Street, and never received any formal art training. Then a leg injury prevented him from working, and he took up sculpting. When his leg healed, he went back to the bakery but vacillated over whether to stay in the family business or take up sculpting full time. Eventually, his heart made the decision for him: he experienced three minor heart attacks where his heart failed, with no medical explanation. By 1991, he was working as a full-time artist.

Maarten seems to have stumbled upon his talent by chance, but then, chance has played a large role in the Schaddelees' lives. When Nadine first saw the Gordon Head house in 1978, she wasn't looking for property. She had planned to accompany a friend who was interested in buying the house, but when the friend had to cancel, Nadine felt she had to keep the appointment. She did, and instantly fell in love with the 1950's bungalow and the property, which once belonged to the Vantreight family. The Schaddelees bought the house and began an intensive five-year renovation process that expanded the house and added a deck, which was walled in to become Maarten's stone and wood carving studios.

His work can be found throughout the city: "Millennium Peace" is a 2,500 kg. marble sculpture currently displayed at Clover Point; "When Peace Comes" was inspired by the Canadian Forces liberation of Holland in World War II and is now displayed in the lobby of the Save On Foods Memorial Centre; his early works were included in part of the Royal B.C. Museums "Whales, The Enduring Legacy" exhibit; and his current commissions include two sculptures for Victoria's Inner Harbour.

"When Peace Comes" has an especially personal connection to Maarten and Nadine. Nadine's father was among the Canadian troops who liberated Holland during the Second World War, including the liberation of the village where Maarten's family lived. In 1955, Maarten and his family emigrated to Victoria. In 1967, Nadine was runner-up for Miss Victoria. Afterwards, she attended the Culinary Arts Ball and Maarten asked her to dance. Eleven days later, they were engaged and five months later the 21 year olds were married. They have two sons, and have been married now for almost forty years, working as a team in what they describe as a labour of love.

(Courtesy Times Colonist)

A Woman of Distinction

BUNCY PAGELY

(Courtesy Buncy Pagely)

Buncy Pagely: 1941 –

When Buncy Pagely was 17 and teaching "survival English" to immigrant women at the local temple, she learned an important lesson: go to the people you want to speak to, because they won't come to you. It's a philosophy that has been very successful during her long and varied volunteer career. She has facilitated workshops across the province to heighten awareness among immigrant women regarding preventative health measures. She has been involved with numerous health, multicultural boards and committees, and received a variety of community, provincial and national awards for her work.

Buncy, who lived in Saanich for 62 years, grew up in a family dedicated to community service. Her grandfather, Battan Singh Beadall, emigrated from India and founded a fuel company in Victoria. He was involved in the establishment of the area's first temple, and he personally financed a four-person trip to Ottawa to meet with Canada's immigration minister in the 1940's. The trip cost $24,000, but was successful in that many East Indians were finally granted landed immigrant status.

Her father, Mahinder Singh Beadall, served as a translator and facilitator for many people new to Canada. He would help people fill out forms, such as immigration papers and visas; Buncy remembers that the family would often receive a phone call whenever a new family had arrived at the airport, and her father would go to help the family settle in.

When she was working at a bank that was situated in an area where there was a large population of recent immigrants, she was often asked to translate, and she soon realized that there was a high proportion of people who lacked an understanding of basic English. So she and a friend began to offer classes at the temple. After work, they taught a group of women how to write their name, count, and catch the bus. It was the beginning of a long and varied career in multiculturalism.

Buncy is a founding member of the Greater Victoria Multicultural Women's Association (GVMWA), a volunteer centre for women and families of all cultural backgrounds. The centre offers educational programs, many of which were geared towards preventative health care. When her niece found a lump during a breast self-exam, Buncy fully realized how important screening is, and how few women (immigrant women in particular) perform such exams. This lead to the founding of her business, Pagely Consulting. As a consultant, she and her husband, Raj, organized a series of 50 cancer awareness workshops across the province to heighten awareness of immigrant and visible minority women about mammograms, breast self-exams, pap tests and nutrition. From 1991 to 1996, there were over 2,000 participants and 200 healthcare professionals involved. From 1995 to 1998, Buncy coordinated 23 Smart Heart Awareness programs, specifically targeting South Asian communities. She applied the same philosophy she had learned when teaching English to the workshops: she held them where people would be most comfortable, whether that was in a Sikh Temple, an Ismali Mosque or another ethnic hall. Sometimes there would be

up to 500 people in a room.

Buncy was a consultant in the development of the Canadian Multicultural Act and the Multicultural Policy for British Columbia. She has also been involved in a study of B.C. hospitals and cross-cultural sensitivity, which examines how various factors may impede health care for people of different cultures. In addition to potential language barriers between staff and patients, many hospitals serve only one type of food, regardless of what the patient is accustomed to eating, which can be detrimental to their recovery.

Currently, Buncy is involved with education health programs for the Songhee's First Nations community. She helped develop the first Diabetes Health Care Centre, and a program called "Healthy Choice," which was delivered to students in elementary, junior and high schools. In 1999, she was elected to the Aboriginal Advisory Panel for the Capital Health Region.

For her many years of volunteering, Buncy Pagely has received awards on many levels. Some of these include the 125th Canada Commemorative Medal, the Citation Rose Award and Citizen of the Year Award from C-FAX and the Honorary Citizen Award from the city of Victoria. In 2005, she became the first Indo-Canadian woman to receive the YM-YWCA Woman of Distinction Lifetime Achievement Award in Canada.

Studying the Cosmos

CHRIS HUNTER

UVIC's McPherson Library (Courtesy University of Victoria)

Chris Hunter

How did the universe begin? How, and when, will it end?

These types of cosmological questions are some of the most difficult and hotly debated topics among both scientists and the general public. Since time immemorial, people have put forth theories about the origins and nature of the universe, but theoretical physics has proved to be an elusive and demanding subject.

Chris Hunter, a former Lambrick Park Secondary student and UVic graduate, is among a select few who was chosen to develop these theories with one of the most brilliant theoretical physicists in history, Dr. Stephen Hawking.

Chris was working part-time at Munro's bookstore in downtown Victoria when Stephen Hawking's bestselling book, *A Brief History of Time*, was released. Like thousands of others, Chris bought the book, but admitted that he didn't wholly understand it at the time. Then, Chris moved to England to enter the year-long pre-doctoral program in theoretical physics at Cambridge University. He listed Hawking as his first choice for a supervisor, but as Hawking only accepts one graduate student a year, the odds that Chris would be the chosen were a long shot. Hawking is considered a leader of the group of physicists who are searching for one unified scientific theory that will explain some of the most difficult cosmological questions ever tackled by scientists, and unlike many scientists, who labour under relative obscurity, Hawking has become a household name among the general public, and is often likened to Albert Einstein and Issac Newton for his tremendous contributions to the field.

While preparing for the interview with the famous physicist, Chris re-read *A Brief History of Time* from cover to cover. The second reading must have done the trick, as Hunter was chosen from among the top physicist students in the world for the coveted position.

Even as a student at Lambrick Park Secondary School, Chris Hunter had excelled in academics. He went on to take a double major in physics and math (arguably the most strenuous academic double major offered) and graduated from UVic in 1994. He earned the Governor General's silver medal for the highest graduating average in all faculties and won the four-year Natural Sciences and Engineering Research Council of Canada (NSERC) grant, worth about $21,000 a year, in recognition of his academic success.

Hunter was also involved in the co-op program at UVic. Some of his four-month co-op positions included work terms at CERN, a particle physics research centre near Geneva, Switzerland; an observatory in Hawaii; and a position with the Triumf research centre at the University of British Columbia.

After he obtained his PhD in general relativity from the University of Cambridge, Chris became a quantitative analyst at BNP Paribas Bank, based in New York. He also became a visiting lecturer in the Mathematics department at Kings College, London, where he is a member of the Financial Mathematics Research Group.

But, it isn't all about black holes and gamma rays for Chris – he also speaks two languages, plays the jazz bass and the piano, and plays tennis and hockey. While he was pursuing his PhD, he played the goalie for the Cambridge B hockey team, a group of Canadian students living abroad.

Construction of Blenkinsop Bridge on the Lochside Regional Trail (Courtesy Saanich Parks and Recreation)

Vancouver Island Technology Park (Courtesy Saanich Planning Department)

1996 - 2005

The most recent decade in Saanich is characterized by a dedication to improving community services and infrastructure. In 2000, Saanich hosted the B.C Games with venues at Cedar Hill Recreation Centre and Saanich Commonwealth Place. These two centres are a large part of the reason Saanich now records over 1,000,000 users of recreation services annually! The LIFE (Leisure Involvement for Everyone) program rolled out in 2004 to assist low income individuals and families enjoy access to Saanich Recreation programs and services. Saanich council dedicated much time and funds to the "safer route to school" program, installing pedestrian traffic signals at seven intersections and completing sidewalks to service elementary and high schools, as well as the UVIC community. To further reinforce public safety, Saanich incorporated new technology to its emergency services with the CREST (Capital Region Emergency Systems Telecommunications) program, which received the Foundation of the Future Award in 2004. Coinciding with the new emergency services was the adoption of a new Municipal Youth Strategy, which helped develop more youth-focused Recreation centres and a skateboard park in Gordon Head. The numerous fatal car accidents involving young people sparked conversation, culminating in a new Speed Watch program in 2004.

Saanich still continues its commitment to preserving the environment and rural community that is its heritage. A Saanich Environmentally Significant Atlas was created, and the first annual Environmental Awards were held in 2000. A new GIS (Geographic Information Systems) mapping service, which allows Saanich residents to build detailed maps of Saanich online, received national recognition for innovation. Urban development continues with the opening of the Vancouver Island Technological Park, as well as approvals for extensive future construction such as Tuscany Village at McKenzie and Shelbourne, and the Cordova Bay Road Project, the result of a twelve year planning process which will include bike lanes, an ornamental brick intersection, landscaping and a separated sidewalk. UVIC continued to expand, and now has a population of more than 18,000 students and receives international recognition for its research facilities.

While we can be sure Saanich will continue to grow in the years to come, residents can expect the development of housing and other facilities, parks and services will strive to preserve a balance of urban and rural living.

The Lady Godiva of Saanich

BRIONY PENN

Briony Penn

Books and articles that discuss worms, huckleberries, mushrooms, broom and salamanders may not be an obvious choice when looking for exciting reading. But Briony Penn has written about all of these things, and her writing is informative, creative and entertaining. She once said that nature writers have reputations as "sexless, earnest sorts of people," and so that is exactly what she avoids – and has avoided very successfully. Her book, *A Walk on the Wild Side*, is a compilation of articles from 10 years of writing columns for Monday Magazine, and was on the BC best sellers list for six months. She also co-authored a book titled *Giving the Land a Voice*.

As an environmentalist, broadcast journalist, illustrator and writer who admits that as a child, she preferred Disney to more serious nature programs, Penn is not above spicing up her pieces if it will make the public more aware of the world around them. In fact, Penn is not above anything – even taking her clothes off in downtown Vancouver

(Courtesy Larry Halverson)

– if it will help her preserve the environment.

Penn's family has a long history on Vancouver Island. Her great-great-grandfather was the first Supreme Court judge in B.C., and her great-grandmother painted many landscapes of an undeveloped Island, paintings that inspire Penn to preserve what remains. She grew up among the Garry oak forests on Christmas Hill; her family, the Bridgmans, have lived there for three generations, since her great-grandfather Arthur Bridgman purchased the property in the early part of the century. Her grandfather, Montague, built a house there in 1937. Rosemary and Dr. Michael Penn, Briony's parents, built their house below the Bridgman home in 1956. Penn first dipped her toe in conservation waters as an eight year old, when she wrote letters trying to save Christmas Hill from high-density development.

Penn spent seven years in Scotland pursuing a graduate degree in geography at the University of Edinburgh, where she met her husband, Donald Gunn. The couple have two children and live in a Victoria home that was scheduled for demolition when Penn saw it. She had it shipped by barge to Salt Spring Island.

Penn helped found the successful Land Conservancy of B.C. and the Garry Oak Meadows Preservation Society. She was also host of the NewVI's Enviro/Mental TV show. But she is probably most famous for her Lady Godiva-like ride through downtown Vancouver in 2001. The ride was a protest against logging on Salt Spring Island, an area that contains some of the last strands of old-growth Douglas fir and Garry oak. Penn helped raise millions to buy the land from Texada Land Corporation; she and other Island women even posed nude for a calendar, which raised over $100,000.

But Texada wouldn't negotiate, so Penn threw off her clothes, donned an ankle-length wig and rode a horse down Vancouver's Howe Street, circling the city block that houses the offices of Texada Land Corp. four times and halting traffic for more than an hour.

Eventually, Penn's ride had the effect that all her credentials and her PhD did not – it grabbed the media's attention – and 32 hectares of Canada's largest Garry oak woodland was protected. Since the first settlers arrived in the 19th century Saanich has experienced a metamorphosis: from forests to farms to suburbia. But if Briony Penn has anything to say about it, there will always be parks and protected areas where future generations can enjoy the old Saanich.

Trivial? Not at all

DAVID MANGA

David Manga

In a world of video games, television and other electronic entertainment, the tenure of the board game as the leading choice of entertainment for youth and adults has been slipping. In fact, in some households the board game is an endangered species; classics like Monopoly are relegated to the back shelves of closets in favour of games like the Sims and Halo 2.

(Courtesy Outset Media)

But David Manga, a young entrepreneur and founder of Outset Media, is working to revive the board game. He believes the old-fashioned board game is capable of teaching some very contemporary skills and values, including strategic thinking, the balance of risk, and decision making. They also offer a cross-generational platform, and while it's a challenge to develop games that a large range of people can play, Outset Media's philosophy is about bringing families together.

Manga founded Outset Media in 1996 after playing Trivial Pursuit and wishing it had more Canadian content – even though the game was designed by Canadians. At the time, David was a student at the University of Ottawa and pursuing a B.A. in economics when he began to gather interesting and obscure Canadian facts from every source he could think of (including cereal boxes) to create his first game. When chartered banks turned down his request for a loan, David,

undaunted, borrowed the money from family and friends. The result was the All-Canadian Trivia Board Game, which has sold more than 100,000 copies and has since been expanded: there is now a French edition, a junior edition and a millennium edition.

The head office of Outset Media is in Commerce Circle in Saanich, where all of the development for the games occurs. In 2001, growing operations required an expansion and the company now has warehouses in Montreal and in Plattsburgh, New York, where the games are distributed internationally.

Since the All-Canadian Trivia game, Outset Media now distributes more than 100 games and 115 puzzles; for the past three years, Outset Media has been ranked by Profit Magazine's PROFIT 100 as one of the fastest-growing companies in Canada. In 2004, David and his team developed Vancouver Islandopoly, a remake of the old classic with a local twist. For example, there is no jail in Islandopoly; instead, players may be sent to the back of the ferry lineup, and instead of a Boardwalk or Park Place, they used Butchart Gardens and the Empress Hotel. The game was also a fundraiser; $2 from the sale of each game went towards the Queen Alexandra Foundation for Children.

Educational games and products are becoming

a large part of Outset Media's business. The Professor Noggin card games sell approximately 200,000 sets a year, and they also deal with jigsaw puzzles and colouring books.

Outset Media places a strong emphasis on customer service. They respond next-day to request for catalogues and quickly fill retailers' order requests; their business practises have been referred to as "under-promise and over-deliver," and Outset Media website declares that "Outset Media's goal is to be the most respected distributor of board games, card games and puzzles to specialty retailers in North America."

David is involved with the Young Entrepreneurs Organization, a club for business owners who are under 40 and doing a minimum of $1 million of sales annually. He received the Young Entrepreneur Award from the Greater Victoria Chamber of Commerce, and was named Manufacturer of the Year by the Vancouver Island Business Excellence Awards. Maclean's magazine declared Manga one of "100 Canadians to Watch."

While David Manga may be in the business of trivia, he's proven that board games are anything but trivial.

This biography has been sponsored by

VICTORIA CHAMBER OF COMMERCE
850 Courtney Street, Victoria, BC V8W 1C4   (250) 383-7191

A Saanich Role Model

RON LOU-POY

(Courtesy University of Victoria)

Ron Lou-Poy

When Ron Lou-Poy was elected the ninth Chancellor of the University of Victoria in 2003, he became the unofficial role model for UVic students and an ambassador for the university. The Chancellor acts as the titular head to the university, and confers degrees to graduates at convocation while serving as an inspiration and model character to these graduates. Ron has travelled to both Nunavut and Beijing to confer degrees to honorary UVic grads, and been the international face that many will associate with Victoria and the university. He won a second term by acclamation that will begin in 2006.

For Ron, a third-generation Victorian and long-time Saanich resident, inspiring by example is nothing new. As a lawyer and philanthropist who has been a member of Kiwanis, president and member of the McPherson Foundation and involved with the Chinese Consolidated Benevolent Association, United Way and Victoria Crime Stoppers, his community involvement has been on going and in-depth. He participated in the fundraising campaign to help raise money to reconstruct the Gate of Harmonious Interest in Victoria's historic Chinatown, and has worked to see the Chinese Cemetery declared a historic site.

Ron grew up in a close extended family with a good understanding of Chinese cultural history. His grandfather emigrated from China in the 1890's and sold silk in the city before he turned to farming. His parents, Harry and Alice, were raised during a period of history in which elementary schools were segregated. When Harry began to attend Grade 8 in an open public school, he was three years older than the other students. He left school shortly after; his wife Alice had left school in Grade 6. Like his father, Harry Lou-Poy became a farmer. He rented land and greenhouses in Victoria and Saanich to grow seasonal vegetables, and opened a store to sell his produce. He and his younger brother Henry developed a successful wholesale operation, called the Pioneer Fruit and Vegetable Company.

Harry Lou-Poy was an active voice against the racial discrimination he had experienced in the community and in schools. He fought against a Victoria school board policy against buying produce from Chinese farmers, and had the satisfaction of seeing the policy later overturned. He also took up the cause of a Chinese driver who was put in jail by Victoria police for a minor speeding infraction.

Though neither Harry nor Alice completed high school, both they and an influential teacher, Lawrie Wallace, encouraged Ron to go to university. He listened to their advice and attended Victoria College, the forerunner to UVic, for two years. He then attended UBC, graduating with a bachelor of commerce in 1957 and a bachelor of laws in 1960. He met his wife May while he was pursuing his law degree (she was a pharmacy student, also attending UBC). They have two children, one of whom graduated from UVic. In 1980, the Lou-Poys moved to Vista Bay Road in Saanich, where they live today.

Ron was hired by Crease and Co. (now Crease, Harman and Company, and the oldest law firm in the province) in 1960. Shortly after making full partner in the mid-1960s, he became one of the first non-white men to be inducted into the Union Club. Two decades later, he stopped attending the club after a vote in which the organization refused to extend memberships to women.

In addition to his election for two terms as the University Chancellor, Ron has served two terms on UVic's Board of Governors (1972 – 74 and 1992 – 95) and was an original director of the UVic Innovation and Development Corporation. The family created the May and Ron Lou-Poy Fund of Excellence in the Faculty of Law, and also contributed more than $270,000 to the University's Harry Lou-Poy Infant and Toddler Centre, which was named in honour of Lou-Poy's father.

Ron's strength of character has not gone unnoticed, either in the community or nationally. He received Canada's highest honour for lifetime achievement when he was appointed to the Order of Canada in 2004. He received an Honorary Doctorate of Laws from UVic in 2000. He is also an Honorary Citizen of Victoria, a recipient of the Community Service Award from the Canadian Bar Association (BC Branch) and the Queen's Golden Jubilee Medal.

As a lawyer, philanthropist and cultural authority, Ron Lou-Poy is an inspiring role model, and UVic is fortunate to have him as Chancellor.

(Courtesy Silken Laumann)

Still Making Waves
SILKEN LAUMANN

Silken Laumann: 1964 –

Elk Lake is as smooth as a mirror, except when Silken Laumann's paddles dip below the surface, fall back and lift, sprinkling water across the surface and creating waves that ripple outwards to the shore.

Laumann, winner of three Olympic medals and a world championship, has trained at Elk Lake for years. She trained there after her leg was so badly broken that she had to be lifted into her boat; she trained there after a drug-test scandal stripped her of the gold medals she won in the Pan American games, and she rows there still, but now as a business-owning mom.

Growing up in Ontario, Laumann's first rowing attempts left her in the water more frequently than on it, but she persisted and learned to love the sport. She and her sister won a bronze medal in the double sculls race in 1984, and she placed seventh in doubles in 1988. In 1990 and 1991 she won the world women's singles sculling title, and the media hailed her as a future gold-medalist.

Then, just ten weeks before the 1992 Olympics, another boat slammed into her scull, breaking her right leg so badly that she required eight surgeries. She spent three weeks in the hospital, where doctors told her that one day she might be able to row recreationally. Ignoring them, she started training as soon as she was released. When she won the bronze medal, she became a Canadian hero.

In 1995, Laumann was on a gold-medal track to the 1996 Olympics when she competed as both an individual and on the quadruple team at the Pan American Games. She won gold in both events, only to find that she tested positive for the banned substance ephedrine, a substance found in the cough and decongestant medication Benadryl.

She had disclosed that she was taking the medication on her drug test and was advised by two team doctors that it was allowed – ephedrine is found in many over-the-counter cold medications – but Laumann and her teammates were stripped of their medals, and Laumann also faced a two-year suspension that would bar her from the next Olympics.

After a month of unpleasantness, during which some people said the rules were unfair and others said Laumann should have known better, she was cleared of the doping charges.

She won silver in Atlanta, not the hoped-for gold, but she still holds a place in the hearts of Canadians. She was named Canada's second female athlete of the Century and has been inducted into the B.C. Sports Hall of Fame; a movie depicting her story was aired on BCTV and the Disney Channel.

Canada became hopeful for a gold medal when Laumann considered competing in the 2000 Sydney games, but she ultimately decided that her family was more important and she announced her retirement in 1999. In 1993 she had married John Wallace, a fellow rower who won a gold medal in 1988, and they have two children, William and Kate, who they are raising in their Cadboro Bay home.

She became a spokesperson for the B.C. Women's Hospital Foundation and became involved in a rowing program for troubled youth. She also founded a business, Silken & Co., to handle her speaking engagements, as she travels all over the world as a motivational speaker. As might be expected of an elite athlete who battled her way back from a potentially career-ending injury to compete against the best in the world, Laumann is still making waves.

Canada's famous, controversial, intoxicating filmmaker
ATOM EGOYAN

Atom Egoyan

Atom Egoyan's first film, *The Lust of the Eunuch*, was shot in 1978 when he was still a student at Mount Douglas High School. Now, as the director of *The Sweet Hereafter* and *Ararat*, he is easily one of the most recognized figures in the Canadian film industry.

Atom's parents, Shushan and Joseph Egoyan, met when they were art students in Cairo, Egypt.

They left to escape the increasingly stifled politics of the region, and moved to Saanich with three-year-old Atom and his younger sister Eve. They opened Ego Interiors, an imported furnishings store, on Fort Street in 1962.

When Ego Interiors burned to the ground in 1990, the insurance adjustor who came to assess the rubble became the inspiration for Atom's fourth film. While *The Adjuster* received lukewarm responses from audiences and critics,

(Courtesy Johnnie Eisen)

some of Atom's films have been extremely successful, and have won some of the top awards in the industry.

His film *The Sweet Hereafter* was an independent, Canadian-made film with a budget of only $4 million. Nonetheless, it was nominated for two Academy Awards: best director and best screenplay adaptation. It was the first time in Oscar history that two Canadians were nominated for best director, the other being James Cameron of the blockbuster production Titanic.

As well as the two Oscar nominations, *The Sweet Hereafter* won three prizes at the Cannes Film Festival, was honored by the National Board of Review, was runner-up at the New York and Los Angeles Film Critics' Awards and appeared on over 250 Ten Best Lists. Atom was named an officer to the Order of Canada in 1999 and received an honorary degree from UVic in 1998.

Atom's sister, Eve Egoyan, also has a degree from UVic, although hers is a BA in Music. As a pianist who specializes in new music and music from the turn of the century, Eve has had to fight to make a name for herself from under the shadow of her famous brother. Her lengthy resume includes studies at the Victoria Conservatory of Music and the Banff Centre of Fine Arts. She released her debut CD, The Things in Between, in 1999. It received glowing reviews from the National Post, the Globe and Mail and other publications.

Atom has never shied away from controversial subjects, from incest to genocide to abortion. He tackled a particularly thorny topic in *Ararat*, a film about the Armenian genocide in 1915. Both his parents and his wife Arsinee Khanjian, who acted in the film, are Armenian. The film caused an uproar: the Turkish government continues to deny that a genocide occurred, and the film was pulled from theatres in Turkey before its release after the distributor received threats from nationalist paramilitary groups and Turkish military and intelligence units. In Canada, the film won several awards, including a Genie Award for best picture.

Atom's most recent movie, *Where the Truth Lies*, is the director's most mainstream production. With a $26 million budget and actors such as Colin Firth, Kevin Bacon and Alison Lohman on the cast, many people feel the movie might win him the Oscar he came so close to in 1997. Some people criticized him for the move towards mainstream film production, and felt that it didn't live up to the sophisticated and complex work he had done in the past, while others praised it for its accessibility.

While *Where the Truth Lies* may be his most accessible movie to date, it is controversial. Adapted from a prize-winning novel by Rupert Holmes, Atom said he wanted the movie to have an intoxicating affect on the viewer, to recreate the hedonism, corruption and moral duplicity of the story. Despite its controversy, it was picked up by several countries for distribution, and was a contender for the Palme d'Or, a top award at the 58th Cannes film festival in 2005 (he won the International Critics Prize for Exotic at the festival in 1994). *Where the Truth Lies* marked his sixth appearance at the Cannes Festival, and in all probability, it won't be his last.

The Pop Princess
NELLY FURTADO

Nelly Furtado: 1979 –

Since Nelly Furtado's album *Whoa! Nelly* was released in 2000, she's been doing a lot of flying and soaring. When her first hit single *I'm like a Bird* won a Grammy in 2002 – the music equivalent of an Oscar – she soared in newspapers across the country, and the brown-haired, bright blue-eyed musician was instantly famous.

Now, the singer, songwriter and mother lives in Toronto, but the pop princess still wears a local crown. Furtado went to high school at Mt. Douglas, and many of the songs on her first album were written in her home in Gordon Head. She wrote "Hey Man" in her bedroom when she was 18, and wrote "Party" while she was working at her summer job, cleaning rooms at the Robin Hood Motel, where her mother once worked.

Furtado began playing piano when she was four,

(Courtesy Island Publishers News Group)

and at the same age, she and her mother performed a duet in front of their church congregation – about 300 people. She described the event as a pivotal moment, when she realized she wanted to be a performer. She played in school bands, learned the ukulele and the trombone and began writing her own songs when she was 12. But unlike many of her peers, Furtado had relatively little show business experience before her first album was released. She rapidly made up for any lack of experience, and has opened for bands like U2, in front of crowds of more than 100,000 people, has performed duets with Elton John and performed on TV specials with Aretha Franklin and Janet Jackson. She won four Juno awards and was nominated for four Grammys in 2002, including best new artist, best pop vocal album, best female pop vocal performance and song of the year. She scooped the award for Best Female pop vocal performance away from veterans such as Janet Jackson and Faith Hill.

Furtado comes back to Saanich frequently to visit her family and perform at the McPherson and Royal Theatres. She speaks three languages, English, Portuguese and Hindi, and has been involved in several fundraising efforts. In May 2002, she sang at UVic's University Centre Auditorium with Victoria's Getting' Higher Choir to raise money for the village Kapasseni in Mozambique; in December of that year, she sang in Johannesburg in South Africa to raise money for the fight against AIDS. More recently, she placed her support behind The Land Conservancy of B.C.'s efforts to have the Sooke Potholes declared a regional park (the land came up in a court-ordered sale in 2003.) Furtado, who says the potholes were one of her favourite swimming spots when she was a teenager, raised the profile of the issue, and brought donations from all over the world. The project has successfully ensured that the 63.5-hectare area is safe from development, and will remain a popular swimming destination.

In September of 2003, Furtado had a baby girl, and Nevis now travels everywhere with her touring parents (her father, Jasper Gahunia, is Furtado's DJ.) Also in 2003, Furtado released her second hit single, *Powerless*, and its accompanying album, *Folklore*. The album was written quickly (she says she wrote some of the songs in less than 10 minutes), but nevertheless, was nominated for four Junos, competing with artists like Sarah McLachlan and Shania Twain, and won the trophy for single of the year with *Powerless*. She says the album, which sold about 397,000 copies, reflects her Canadian-Portuguese heritage. She is currently in the process of recording a third album, suggesting that Nelly will be soaring for many years to come.

A Rink Rat in Saanich

JOHN BATE

John Bate

John Bate believes that having a fun side to balance the serious or business side of life is a necessity. From childhood to retirement, at work or at home, the lengths John goes to achieve this balance makes him one of Saanich's and Victoria's most colourful figures.

John grew up in Vancouver's East End, and spent much of his youth inside the old Vancouver Forum where he and his buddies were self-described "rink rats." Though the boys were sneaking into most Forum events, John befriended the centre manager, Dave Dauphinee, who gave John his first glimpse of how to run a successful arena.

While John is more recognized for his work off the ice, as manager of the former Victoria Memorial Arena and the Christmas Elf of Candy Cane Lane, John had a career on the ice as well. He performed with the Ice Capades during the 1950s, after his natural gift for comedy won him the role of a clown without ever having worn figure skates.

John met Marilyn, his wife and former teammate, while on tour with the Ice Capades. The pair travelled the world with the show before settling on Vancouver Island. While on tour, John proved again and again why he was given

(Courtesy Saanich News)

the role of a clown. In Russia, he led Moscow police on a chase through the city one evening before they finally cornered him atop a bridge and took him to the U.S. Embassy. He was also known to shock the press by arriving at events in unusual ways, like the morning in Portland when he dropped into a press conference suspended from a window-washer's harness. Back in Canada the jokes continued; he once filled the arena press box with straw, fresh manure and live chickens after a journalist called his arena the Barn on Blanshard. Even his friends aren't safe. John has been known to emerge from golf course ponds dressed in scuba gear to serve his surprised buddies with a cold beer.

John's first job at the Memorial Arena was assistant manager under Jack Morgan from 1961 until 1984. When Jack retired, John took over management of the arena, Crystal Pool, Royal Athletic Park, the McPherson Playhouse and the Royal Theatre, as well as Thetis Lake Park. John ran a tight ship at the Memorial Arena, and no one knew about or took more pride in the building than he did. His office was decorated with autographed photos of such diverse stars as Celine Dion, Wilf Chamberlain and the San Diego Chicken, and under his management the arena welcomed musicians Tina Turner, the Beach Boys and Duke Ellington, and sports greats like John McEnroe, Bobby Hall and

Wayne Gretzky. In 1989 John was awarded the first Dave Dauphinee trophy (named for his old mentor from the Forum) in recognition of his services to the community. It is fitting that John's retirement from the centre in 1997 coincided with its demolition later that year.

John's role in the community was by no means restricted to his work at the arena. What began as an idea at a neighbourhood summer barbecue in 1969 would turn into one of Saanich's brightest Christmas attractions: Candy Cane Lane. John and Marilyn began by decorating the big tree in front of their house on Tattersall Drive and handing out candy canes to children passing by as well as their own children, David and Lisa. They added more decorations each year until the last light-up in 1999. After three decades of decorating, the Bate's winter wonderland included snowmen and Santa, reindeer, and John's personal favourite, a replica ice rink—complete with Zamboni. John would usually be dressed up as an elf, swinging from the branches of the tree that started it all. After Candy Cane Lane's last season, John and Marilyn gave the majority of their decorations to Rick Church and Lisa Ferguson who promised to carry on the holiday tradition at their home in Colwood.

Even though the Memorial Arena has been replaced by the Save-On-Foods Memorial Centre, and the lights have dimmed on Candy Cane Lane, John is still bringing his sense of fun to the community. In his latest role as volunteer chair of the Victoria Sports Hall of Fame, he has helped raise funds for a first-class memorabilia display. He also made sure no one forgets the old Memorial Arena by dismantling the old penalty box and preserving it in the new centre.

(Courtesy University of Victoria)

An Elegy to an Earlier Saanich
PHILIP KEVIN PAUL

Philip Kevin Paul: 1971 –

Kevin Paul has been described as the young poet with the voice of an elder, and a conversationalist of culture. He is both a writer and a boxer, and while the craft and the sport may appear to be contradictory, in Kevin, they work together to bring balance.

Kevin is dedicated to preserving what is at risk of being lost, and to live in a way that both cherishes and celebrates the natural environment.

The award-winning poet, boxer and teacher is also the only person of his generation who knows how to speak SENCOTEN, the native language of the WSA,NEC Indians on the Saanich Peninsula. He learned the language from his grandmother. His grandfather worked to create the alphabet of the language that now only a few dozen people can speak.

He was raised in a close-knit family who were dedicated to the Saanich language, traditions and territory. His father was Chief Philip Paul, an internationally known indigenous rights activist and co-founder of the union of B.C. Indian Chiefs. He was well known for his efforts at improving native education and establishing a native-run school on the Tsartlip Reserve, and his name appeared frequently as a spokesperson for the band, protesting and setting up blockades to get the school. He was also a vocal opponent of the Meech Lake Accord

While it isn't uncommon for people today to live in many different houses, communities and even countries during their lifetime, Kevin has lived in the same home and on the same 24 acres since he was born there, and he plans to remain there until the day he dies. His three brothers and their families also live on the land. In an interview, Kevin once said, "The joke in Saanich is if someone asks, 'Do you live far away from your relatives?' you go, 'Yeah, a mile.'"

Kevin learned discipline early: as a lightweight boxer, he often woke before dawn to go for training runs, regardless of the weather. His hard work paid off; he was once ranked fifth in B.C. and thirteenth in Canada. He has brought the same discipline to his writing – his first collection of poems, Taking the Names Down from the Hill, won the Dorothy Livesay Poetry Prize in 2004 for the best book of poetry by a B.C. author. The book began as a project to travel across the Saanich territory, and in an interview, he said that it was an elegy for his parents and for the old names and ideals of Saanich.

After graduating with a B.A. in writing and English from UVic in 2003, Paul is now pursuing a Masters in writing; he is also a sessional professor at the university. He has worked with UVic's linguistics department to translate and preserve local stories, and also with the Institute for Ocean Sciences to correlate Saanich place names.

Kevin Paul is able to bring the discipline of a boxer and the focus of a writer to the task of ensuring that what he was taught about home and community will be passed on to other generations. The traditions, stories and culture of an earlier Saanich are in the hands of a very capable steward.

Saying "YES" to Science
DAVE GARRISON & SHANNON HUNT

Dave Garrison

Shannon Hunt

To produce a cyclone in a soda bottle, you need:

-Two plastic pop bottles, one ¾ full of water
-Duct tape
-A drill

To produce a national, award-winning science magazine for kids, you need:

-Dave Garrison
-Shannon Hunt
-Determination, innovation and a lot of hard work

When Dave Garrison and Shannon Hunt met at UVic's student paper, it was the beginning of a cyclone, except their tornado has destroyed the stereotypes that science is boring and difficult, and instead, has left a trail of award-winning magazines that have fascinated and informed children for almost 10 years.

Despite flooded basement offices, hours of overtime and the obstacles that inevitably accompany the launch of a business from scratch, Garrison and Hunt will celebrate the 10th anniversary of their bimonthly publication, *YES Mag: Canada's Science Magazine For Kids*, in May of 2006. The magazine is aimed at 8 to 14 year olds, and currently has 22,000 subscribers from all over the world, including New Zealand and Kazakhstan.

The subjects covered in *YES Mag* vary from mad cow disease, to how insects breathe, to how nature is adapting to global warming. It includes projects that can be done at home, like how to make a mummy or a soda-bottle cyclone. There is also a section for reader-reviewed, science-related products, such as books or computer software, where youth can see their name and photo printed next to their review.

The founders of *YES Mag* didn't have a lot of writing or business experience when they launched the magazine. Garrison had graduated with a bachelor of engineering degree in 1994, and Hunt had a masters degree in history. She had some journalism experience writing for the Gulf Island's Driftwood newspaper (she lived on Pender Island until she moved to Victoria to attend UVic) and he had worked on an engineering newsletter. They met in 1994 when he was a co-

(Courtesy University of Victoria)

editor and she was a writer for the Martlet.

Garrison had worked for a summer as the program director of UVic's Science Venture summer camp in 1992, where he got a first-hand look at how enthusiastic kids can be about science. Hunt had always wanted to write for kids, and writing about science appealed to her because she hadn't enjoyed it much when she was young. A magazine was a chance to show kids that science was neither a geeky nor a difficult subject.

Using a combination of Hunt's savings and loans from parents (a total of $60,000), and without the help of government subsidies, they turned the basement of their Saanich home into an office. The first two issues were written almost entirely by Hunt, while Garrison handled the marketing and publishing. When it came time for subscription renewal drives, they bribed their family and friends with pizza and held late-night envelope lick-and-stick evenings. Since then, the staff has grown from two to six full-time members and many freelance contributors. They've continued to grow while remaining

relatively logo free; unlike most publications, which rely on advertising for survival, YES Mag usually has only one or two advertisements per 32 pages of information.

The product of their gamble and hard work received almost immediate recognition: YES Mag won the Eve Savoury Award a year after the first issue was produced. In 1999, it was a finalist for the BC Magazine of the Year award, and in 2001, it won the $10,000 Michael Smith Award. In 2000, the year they married, Garrison and Hunt were named one of "100 young Canadians to watch" by Maclean's Magazine.

As for the future, they are in the process of starting another science magazine for younger children. They've authored two books, *International Space Station* and *Fantastic Feats and Failures*," (both were nominated for the Silver Birch Award) and are working on a third. And, of course, they will continue to produce the magazine that offers fun facts and riveting science to children around the world.

Improving the Odds
MATT UNDERWOOD

(Courtesy Linda Elliott)

Matt Underwood: d. 1998, age 25

In December of 1995, 23-year-old Matt Underwood had plans. The Tsawout native was a talented lacrosse player and coach, and was working towards playing for the Victoria Shamrocks. He wanted to go to UVic to complete a degree in education. And, in August, he was going to marry his fiancée.

But all of Underwood's plans were put on hold when he was admitted to the hospital with only a third of the red blood cells of a healthy person. He

was diagnosed with chronic myeloid leukaemia (CML), a form of cancer in which cancerous cells gradually replace the healthy blood cells in bone marrow. At the time, the odds of finding a bone-marrow transplant – Underwood's best chance for survival – were 1 in 10,000.

The treatment of CML usually involves intense chemotherapy and radiation to kill all bone marrow cells – cancerous and healthy – before a bone marrow transplant. But no one in Underwood's extended family was a match. Ninety per cent of the members in the national bone marrow registry are Caucasian, and the chances of finding a matching donor were highest among Matt's own ethnic group. Fewer than 900 of Canada's 141,000 registered donors on the national registry are of native descent.

So Underwood made a new goal. He took the energy he once gave to sports, and poured it into raising awareness of the Unrelated Bone Marrow Registry Program run by the Canadian Red Cross society. He turned his 24th birthday party into a celebration/bone marrow information session. Four hundred people attended the event, held at the Lau-Wel-New Tribal School, and 450 people signed up to the Red Cross bone marrow registry.

Next, Underwood turned his attentions to the North American Indigenous Games, during which 8,000 aboriginal athletes and cultural performers would be flooding Victoria. It wasn't his first time at the Games; when he was 17 and a member of the Junior A Esquimalt Eagles lacrosse club, he represented the province at the Indigenous Games in Edmonton, when the B.C. team won a bronze medal. Now, instead of playing, he was on the sidelines, raising awareness through an information booth staffed by volunteers. Nearly 200 people registered at the Games, although none of them were a match to Underwood.

Despite the lack of donors, Underwood remained optimistic that he would beat the disease, and for a time, it seemed he would. His fiancée, Dawn Frank, became pregnant, despite the fertility-suppressing drugs Underwood was taking to treat his cancer. It was considered little less than a miracle when their baby, named Bridgette, was born on October 17, 1997.

Sixth months after Bridgette's birth, Underwood went to Vancouver and underwent a month-long course of chemotherapy that appeared to put his cancer into remission, and he was able to return home with Dawn and their young daughter.

Finally, after a two-year search, a bone-marrow donor was found in June of 1998. The donor was not a perfect match for Underwood, which meant there could be complications, but it was his best chance at beating the leukemia, and his youth increased the odds that the transplant would be successful. Tragically, three weeks after his bone marrow transplant, complications did arise, and the donor cells rejected his body. He died in 1998, when he was only 25. Six hundred people attended his funeral.

Matt (left) with his best friend Nick Claxton
(Courtesy Linda Elliott)

During his fight with cancer, Underwood made national headlines publicising the long odds faced by North American aboriginals who require bone marrow transplants. As a result of his efforts, the odds faced by the next leukemia patient might be a good deal shorter than the 1 in 10,000 odds that Underwood faced in 1995.

This biography has been sponsored by
Ida Chong, MLA
Oak Bay-Gordon Head
223 – 3930 Shelbourne Street, Victoria, BC V8P 5P6   Phone: 473-8528

Making a Global Difference
DELL MARIE WERGELAND

(Courtesy D. Wergeland)

Dell Marie Wergeland

In a crowded warehouse in Esquimalt, computer parts, school desks and hospital beds compete for space. Stacks of clearly labelled boxes reach the ceiling; bags of teddy bears and blankets rest on top. In one room, a wall serves as a showcase for photos of people and places from all over the world. One picture depicts a group of children in an African refugee camp, where buildings with straw roofs rest on dirt and stand against a hazy blue sky. Most of the children are smiling; one little girl is wearing pink shoes and a bright white t-shirt. It wouldn't seem unusual to a Canadian, but these bright clothes and smiles stand out in a landscape of dust and scarcity.

It's photos like these that remind coordinator Dell Wergeland and the team of volunteers at the Compassionate Resource Warehouse (CRW) why they devote so many hours of their time to the warehouse and its contents. The CRW is an international aid organization that collects donated goods from hospitals, schools, businesses and individuals and sends it to locations around the globe. While most international aid organizations specialize in only one area, such as medical supplies or clothing, the CRW collects a wide variety of goods – from blankets to computers to discontinued vitamins – and can provide almost everything a small community needs in one shipment.

The CRW began in 1999 after long-time Saanich resident Dell went as a volunteer to Honduras. Hurricane Mitch had recently destroyed many people's homes and sources of livelihood, and she and her husband, Vic Wergeland, and her brother-in-law, Saanich councillor Leif Wergeland, were travelling to a refugee camp to volunteer. Both Vic and Leif had been on building projects before, but it was Dell's first experience in a developing country. She was stunned by how little the people had, even though it was supposed to be a relatively well-supplied refugee camp, and she realized that Canadians have a great capacity to help people overseas.

When the Wergelands returned to Canada, they decided they would do more to help the community in Honduras. Though Dell had been planning to go back to work full-time, she decided to delay her return until she had gathered enough donations to fill a forty-foot container. E.Y. Construction donated 5,000 square feet of warehouse space to the cause, and donations began to slowly trickle in. It took more than a year to fill the container, but when it was finally shipped in September of 2000, Wergeland realized that she had found her full-time occupation: volunteer coordinator.

Dell graduated from Belmont High School and then attended the Royal Jubilee Hospital's nurses training programme. She married Vic Wergeland in 1975, and they moved to Saanich in 1980, where they continue to live today. Before her trip to Honduras, she thought she would return to her former occupation, working with seniors. While she never returned to paid work with seniors, she did recruit many of them as volunteers for the warehouse.

When the CRW receives a request from a relief organization, such as World Relief or Universal Aid, Dell ensures that the materials sent are appropriate. For example, after the tsunami struck Asia in December of 2004, many aid organizations were scrambling to collect donations, and some sent inappropriate items, like winter jackets. Dell's careful organization ensured that the people who received a CRW shipment were able to utilize all of the goods sent.

The CRW has grown rapidly since its inception in 1999, and after a successful fundraising campaign, was able to purchase the warehouse space. The charity shipped 42 containers in 2004, and in December of that year, Dell and CRW volunteers celebrated their 100th shipment. There are currently six people on the board of directors, 10 on the operating committee, and 125 volunteers, who wash clothing, prepare computers, and transport heavy hospital beds from the donor's space to the warehouse.

Though Dell is the driving force behind the CRW, she is quick to point out that it's the dedication and expertise of the volunteers that keep it running. As much as possible, she tries to let people choose tasks that incorporate their own interests, and her willingness to perform the tasks no one else likes to do has been a large part of the charity's success. She maintains that when people realize they can make a difference with a small action, they will realize they can make a difference globally – and that's the motivation that keeps Dell and her volunteers working hard year after year.

This biography has been sponsored by a Supporter of the **Compassionate Warehouse**

Shoot for Peace

STEVE NASH

(Courtesy Steve Nash Foundation)

Steve Nash: 1974 -

Steve Nash is famous. Very famous. If you type his name into an internet search engine, you will get back more than 1,920,000 responses, and that number increases almost weekly. You will learn that he graduated from Santa Clara University in 1996 and was immediately drafted by the Phoenix Suns; that he was picked up by the Dallas Mavericks in 1998, where he went on to become a two-time All-Star in 2002 and 2003. Then, back with the Suns, he signed a $65 million dollar (U.S.) contract and became the sixth-highest paid player in the NBA. In 2005, he received the official crown of the world of basketball, when he became only the second international player to receive the NBA's Most Valuable Player award.

You can learn a lot more about Steve than just

his basketball stats, too. You can find out what his favourite book is (*Catcher in the Rye*), where he was born (Johannesburg, South Africa, on February 7, 1974) and that he admires Mahatma Gandhi, "because he is constantly searching for truth".

You will also learn that Steve was raised in Saanich. His parents, John and Jean, met in England and moved to South Africa. Shortly after Steve was born, the family moved to Regina, then to Vancouver before finally settling in Saanich. Steve graduated from St. Michaels University School and was awarded a scholarship to Santa Clara University in California.

According to many of his team mates and coaches, Steve is an extremely principled player. After he read Naomi Klein's anti-globalization book No Logo, which includes several chapters blasting one of the NBA's most intimate bedfellows, logo-centric sneaker companies, he turned down several lucrative endorsement offerings. When war was declared in Iraq in 2002, he wore a T-shirt to an NBA All-Star game that read, "No War. Shoot for Peace."

Although his childhood hero was Wayne Gretsky and his first love was hockey, when he started playing basketball at age thirteen it quickly became a passion. When he played on the 2000 Canadian Olympic Team, he led the team to its "shocking" victory over Australia and his presence gave people hope that Canada would finally bring home a medal.

According to Craig Daniels from the Toronto Sun, Steve has applied "defibrillator paddles to the sport of basketball in Canada." In a country where hockey is undeniably the most popular sport, he has been credited with making it more appealing to youth and improving Canada's reputation on the international scene.

Canada was ultimately defeated by France (who went on to win the silver medal) and settled in seventh place. But many people say the team's performance improved Canada's image and gave many youth – who used to wear nothing but American players' jerseys – new pride in Canadian basketball.

Back when Steve was a teenager in Saanich, dribbling his ball to school, and even when he was the 15th player chosen in the draft, it's unlikely that many people predicated that his low-key, hard-working approach would one day earn him basketball's most coveted award. After all, in 1995, Sports Illustrated profiled Steve when he was still a student at Santa Clara, and they called him "Victoria's secret." Less than a decade later, "Victoria's secret" has become one of the game's biggest stars. The fact that the 6'3", 195-pound point guard has been so successful in a sport dominated by larger and stronger players speaks to Steve's extraordinary ability, and makes his accomplishments that much more remarkable.

Leading the New Generation of Business Leaders

SHONA SINCLAIR

(Courtesy S. Sinclair)

Shona Sinclair: 1983 –

When she was a student at Mount Douglas Sr. Secondary, Shona Sinclair led the team of young entrepreneurs that won the 2001 B.C. Junior Achievement Student Ventures Competition. For their project, the students researched and developed a line of school clothing that they called "Mount Doug Wear 2000-2001." Their marketing campaign, which included a fashion show and a web page, targeted all students, staff and families associated with the school. Sales from the clothing line reached $42,000 in five weeks, catapulting the team into first place. The win provided Shona with valuable experience and netted her the Evelyn Ruskin Junior Achievement Award, a national scholarship worth $1,000. The win also made Mount Doug the first Victoria school to claim top honours in the six-year history of the competition.

The annual award is sponsored by CIBC to encourage enterprising high school students to learn about business by starting their own, and is intended to provide hands-on experience that will better prepare grade 11 and 12 students for the job market – and Shona has done just that.

After high school, she enrolled in the business program at the University of Victoria, where her experience at Mount Doug proved to be very worthwhile. In 2002, she was chosen out of 500 applicants to be one of three B.C. youths and one of 35 Canadian youths to participate in Global Vision's Junior Team Canada Program. The three-week program was part of an economic trade mission to Guangzhou, Hong Kong, the Philippines and Shanghai, and is dedicated to providing youth ages 16 – 25 with the skills, experience and knowledge necessary to become the new generation of business leaders. As a result of her participation on Junior Team Canada, Minister Pierre Pettigrew invited Shona to join a

Team Canada trade mission to Africa in 2002.

The previous Spring, she had participated in Junior Team Canada's Training Centre in Vancouver. This involved case study presentation competitions and networking sessions with prominent community businesses. After it was over, she decided that she would like to do the same thing on an international scale, and applied to the Asia mission. She was accepted in early July, which gave her only five weeks to fundraise the $4,000 required for her participation in the trip.

Shona was under a tight deadline for raising the money, and the program also specifies that students must be sponsored by the trade sector that they had chosen to represent. She had chosen the B.C. forestry and construction sector, particularly companies dealing in softwood lumber because of the recent trade debates occurring between Canada and the United States. She then created marketing packages and made multiple phone calls. In the five weeks, she not only raised the necessary amount, but raised an additional $4,400, making the total amount raised $8,400. Her sponsors included the Asia Pacific Foundation of Canada, TimberWest Corporation and the University of Victoria.

In Asia, she and other students met with business and government leaders to showcase their Canadian sponsors' products and services. She researched market opportunities and contact information for local forestry and construction

companies interested in doing business in China. The students were also able to sit in on press conferences in each city they visited. They were able to participate through the aid of a translator, and it encouraged Shona to study more languages. When she returned to Canada, she studied both Latin and Spanish.

Since her trip to Asia, Shona has followed up on the connections she made during her fundraising and has since been invited to sit in on certain trade negotiations and presentations. In an interview conducted shortly after her return, she said that she has continued to learn from her sponsors, and this has been as rewarding as the experience she gained overseas.

In recognition of her leadership and excellence in international studies and contributions to B.C.'s export community, Shona won the B.C. Export Award for International Business Studies in 2004. Presented by the Ministry of Small business and Economic Development and the B.C. division of Canadian Manufactures Exports, the award mentioned her four-month co-op work term with Export Development Canada and the Junior Team Canada Trade Mission. In the fall of 2005 Shona began law school at the University of British Columbia

Shona's past achievements, as reflected on her resume, vouch for her future, where her contributions to the business community and number of awards will only continue to grow.

This biography has been sponsored by

VICTORIA CHAMBER OF COMMERCE
850 Courtney Street, Victoria, BC V8W 1C4   (250) 383-7191

Service Above Self

ROTARY INTERNATIONAL

ROTARY is an organization of business and professional leaders united worldwide, who provide humanitarian service, encourage high ethical standards in all vocations, and help build goodwill and peace in the world.

ROTARY is the world's first service club. It was founded in Chicago in 1905 and it became International when the Winnipeg Rotary club was chartered in 1912.

ROTARY is now over 1.2 million service-minded men and women belonging to over 32,000 Rotary clubs in 168 countries around the world. There are 13 Rotary clubs in Greater Victoria, 3 are in Saanich.

ROTARIANS meet weekly for fellowship and interesting and informative programs dealing with topics of local and global importance. Membership is by invitation and reflects a wide cross-section of community representation.

ROTARIANS plan and carry out a remarkable variety of humanitarian, educational, and cultural exchange programs that touch people's lives in their local communities and our world community.

ROTARY is The Rotary Foundation, which each year provides some US$102 million for international scholarships, cultural exchanges, and humanitarian projects large and small that improve the quality of life for millions of people.

ROTARY is compassion for the underprivileged, the ill and the disabled, many of whom are beneficiaries of over 50,000 service projects conducted by Rotary clubs throughout the world.

ROTARY adds fulfillment each year to the lives of more than 800 young people of secondary school age as they live and study in countries other than their own. In addition, more than 1000 ambassadorial scholars attend universities throughout the world to further Rotary's goal of "Peace Through World Understanding"

ROTARY is PolioPlus, Rotary's commitment to work with national and international health organizations on the goal of polio eradication. By 2005, Rotary's 100th anniversary, more than one-half billion children in developing nations have been immunized against polio through PolioPlus grants with the involvement of many Rotary volunteers.

ROTARY IS

SERVICE ABOVE SELF

The Rotary Clubs of Saanich

If you would like to make a difference in your own community and the world community at large, contact one of the following;

The Rotary Club of Saanich

Formed in 1958, this evening Club meets at 6:15 p.m. every Monday at the University Club, UVIC.

If you would like more information on Rotary and/or the Rotary Club of Saanich, please call Bill Bryant at 479-7757.

The Rotary Club of Royal Oak (Centennial)

This Club was formed at midnight January 1st. 2000 and meets for lunch at noon every Monday at the Royal Oak Golf Club.

If you would like more information on Rotary and/or The Royal Oak Centennial Club, please call John Saunders at 743-4831.

The Saanich Sunrise Rotary Club

Meets for breakfast every Tuesday morning at 7:00 a.m. at the de Dutch Pannekoek House at Quadra and McKenzie.

If you would like more information on Rotary and/or the Saanich Sunrise Rotary Club, please contact Jan Brister at 381-2389.

Index of Biographies